P9-DHI-485

Courtesy: Newport Historical Society

Credits

Credit must be given to the Preservation Society of Newport County and the Newport Restoration Foundation whose continued efforts to preserve the architectural heritage of Newport have been an important factor in the necessity for this revised edition. Again, the above organizations and the Newport Historical Society have been most generous in making records and information available. Thanks also goes to Richard Harrington for his carefully considered suggestions and corrections to the first edition. Credit for work on the revised edition goes to Jenniffer Gilmore for assistance in the preparation of written material, and to Sarah Spongberg for her skilled efforts in dealing with the mountains of photographic lab work.

ISBN-0-912210-02-8

Catboat Press
Box 673
Newport, Rhode Island 02840

DESIGNED BY
Constance Mussells *Medium Well Done*
Composition by *Typesetting Service Company*,
Printing by *Foremost Lithograph Company*

NEWPORT
A TOUR GUIDE

REVISED EDITION

text by A.L. Randall
photographs by R.P. Foley

revised second edition
photographs & text by R.P. Foley

Contents

Foreword

This Tour Guide fills a gap in Newport literature. Several guides have been written, but none since restoration swept the city. In this pictoral guide to Newport we have presented a cross-section of Newport's diverse architectural heritage. We have not included every house and may have overlooked some that should have been included.

We have tried to be as accurate as possible in furnishing information but the records are often conflicting and confusing. Some dates can only be approximated and house names have been arbitrarily assigned over the years. Frequently, facts come to light which completely change the dating and history of a house.

The photographs show the houses as they are today. In some cases, even in the midst of resotration. This, in our opinion, is part of the story.

We have set up the guide in walking tours, where possible, with a map and pictures and commentary on each structure. There is also a section on the rest of Aquidneck Island and a list of suggested reading.

We should point out that since this is a guide to a living community it is important to respect the privacy of the owners of these houses.

We hope this guide will provide the reader with as much pleasure as we have had in putting it together.

Avanti!

A.L.R.

Introduction to Revised Edition

In this revised edition of *Newport — A Tour Guide*, an attempt has been made to reflect some of the continuing changes Newport has experienced over the past five years. Buildings have been added to all of the original seven tours and a new eighth tour has been included. The new tour encompasses the waterfront which was briefly noted in the "Other Points of Interest" section of the first edition. In five years this area has been developed with a fairly sympathetic hand until it has become one of the focal points of the city. One can only trust the further inevitable development of the waterfront will continue to reflect the natural beauty of the harbor and the long traditions it represents.

It has been difficult revising these tours. It all seems quite simple until the final check is made on foot over the actual streets. Suddenly there seems to be an endless number of interesting buildings which should be noted and included. There are any number of corners to be turned, streets to pursue and entire areas to awaken people to. Limits are necessary and essential to the concept of this book — this is an introductory guide to Newport and its architecture and is by no means complete. Turn the corner, ponder a building and seek out areas not included — the enjoyment of discovery is there.

R.P.F.

Key to the Maps

The key map shown opposite indicates the location of seven of the eight tours. Tour 5 along Bellevue Avenue and Ocean Drive is self-evident. Each tour map indicates a starting point with an asterisk where parking is usually available. The numbers on the maps refer to the number of the house described with a photograph and text in each tour. The houses are numbered in the order seen by following the footpath on the map. Small cross streets have been eliminated in some cases to avoid a confusion of lines on the maps.

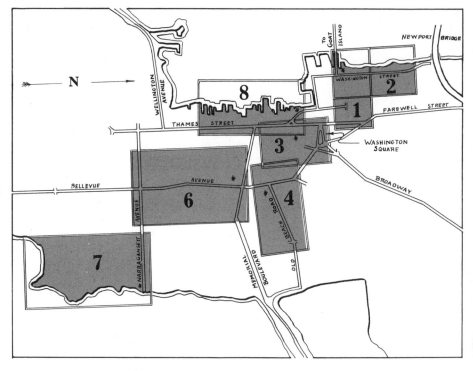

Introduction

Newport, which lies along the southernmost tip of Aquidneck Island, was settled in 1639 by a handful of men. These men were greatly impressed by the natural assets of the harbor and the verdure of the surrounding area. The men, whose names grace many of our streets today—Easton, Coggeshall, Coddington, Clarke, Bull, among others—incorporated and began work by laying out the town. The first house, built by Easton, was on Farewell Street. Others followed shortly. As more room was needed, the settlement expanded southward along Thames Street. Easton's Point was eventually divided into house lots. The harbor which had attracted Easton when he sailed down the bay on his discovery mission proved to be the basis for galloping commercial growth. By the mid-18th century Newport was the most prosperous seaport on the eastern coast. The prosperity brought the usual cultural adjuncts along with it. Distinguished men and women joined the wealthy merchants. Craftsmen produced the best furniture, silver, pewter and clocks in the colonies to adorn the homes of these early Newport residents. Artists were attracted by the handsome commissions proferred to them. The customs and attributes of Newport were recorded for posterity by learned men. Bishop Berkeley and Ezra Stiles were only two of these 18th century scholars who were particularly fond of Newport. Stiles, who preached in the Second Congregational Church on Clarke Street, kept extensive and valuable notes on the affairs of the city.

When British and American relations began to fester, Newporters were fierce in the protection of their liberty. They gained the honor of making the first overt American move against the British when in July, 1769, a party of men went out into the bay and destroyed the British sloop "Liberty." When open hostilities were close at hand, the British occupied Newport. This occupation lasted from December, 1776 until October, 1779. During their stay on the island, the British devastated houses, farms and commercial buildings. Over 500 buildings were ultimately destroyed for firewood. The churches and public buildings were used for barracks or riding academies. Private homes were confiscated to garrison the troops and staff. When the British were finally routed, Newport was in a state of total collapse. It is no wonder that the arrival of the French allies within the year elicited such enthusiasm. The French, although they proved to be disappointing on the battleground, were cherished by Newporters, and the legends of their stay live on and on.

The set-back Newport suffered from the Revolutions lasted many years. The War of 1812 wiped out the slight recovery the city had made and it wasn't until the mid-19th century that the city was able to make its come-back. After several years of such straits that not a single house was built, tourism came to the rescue. Newport had been a favorite resort of the Southern gentry since the early 18th century. Now, as thoughts of war faded into the distance, this same class of people began to trickle back to Newport. Boardinghouses and hotels were opened to stem the tide of visitors. Before long, the visitors became residents. New houses were once again built and by 1850, the rush for land was on. The city once again expanded southward, this time along Bellevue Avenue. The age of Newport as a "summer colony" had arrived. The houses were not the simple homes for elegant living, built by the commercial princes of the 19th century. Life came back to the whole city, prosperity returned and a new influx of talent tapped the cultural dowry of the colonial city. By the turn of the century, Newport was once again, despite her small size, a giant among cities.

The twentieth century brought the "gilded age" of Newport to a close, but the city continues to thrive. Today Newport is known world-wide in many respects. It was the scene of the first Jazz Festival, it has the privilege of providing the America's Cup race course.

Most of all, however, it has its heritage which should never be underemphasized. From this heritage springs the most diversified assortment of houses found anywhere. Not only does Newport contain more colonial houses than any other city in the country, it has 19th and 20th century houses of every known variety. In recent years, this unique architectural inheritance has become a matter of public interest. Groups, first organized by only a dedicated minority, now have full community response to their preservation efforts. The Preservation Society of Newport County, founded in 1945, has been single-handedly responsible for saving several mansions and colonial houses from an odious end. These houses have been repaired or restored, furnished and opened to the public. Operation Clapboard, originally conceived in 1963, has approached preservation from another angle. Set up chiefly as a clearing-house, it makes information available to those interested in restoring a colonial home. Occasionally, a threatened home is purchased by the organization but owner-restoration is their primary goal. So far, the effort has been successful beyond anyone's expectations, and the little acorn emblem, symbolizing strength, adorns many a house. The atmosphere created by these early efforts paved the way for larger endeavors. Newport Restoration Foundation, also a non-profit organization, is financed by private funds. This organization buys and restores the house itself and eventually the houses will be made available for rental or museum purposes.

Newport, both past and future, has a unique place in the history of American cities. It has unlimited possibilities ahead, but probably its most salient attraction is the rich heritage it leaves in its wake.

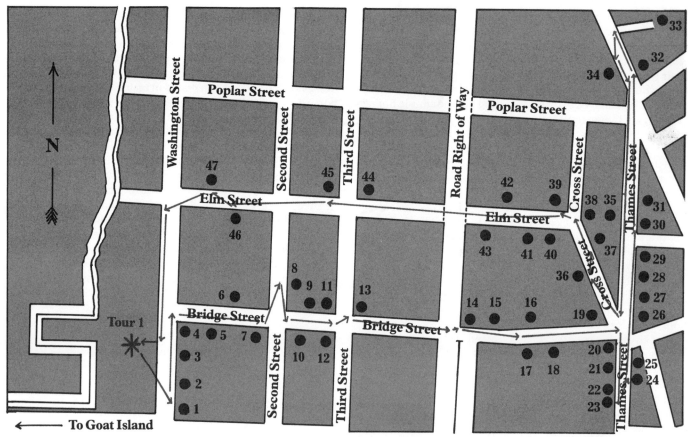

N

Washington Street

Poplar Street

Second Street

Third Street

Road Right of Way

Poplar Street

Cross Street

Thames Street

33

32

34

Elm Street

47

45

44

42

39

38 35

31

30

Elm Street

46

43

41 40

37

8

9 11

13

36

Cross Street

29

28

6

14 15 16

27

Bridge Street

19

26

Tour 1

4 5 7

Bridge Street

20

3

Second Street

10 12

Third Street

17 18

25

2

21

24

1

22

23

Thames Street

To Goat Island

10

Tour 1
The Point —
Bridge Street

To enjoy the flavor of this tour, one must imagine a flourishing 18th century mercantile community. The natural depth of the harbor on the Bay side and the quiet waters of the "Cove" on the South, long since filled in, made the area a natural location for the homes of those who earned their living from the sea. Washington Street was the site of some of the finest homes of the Colonies, built by merchants who were already wealthy and imbued with good taste when they came to Newport. Bridge Street, then known as Shipwright Street, faced on the "Cove" and it was here that the craftsmen involved in fitting out the ships first set up their shops and built their homes. It was a simple matter to deliver ship cabinetwork directly from one's back door on the "Cove." Later Bridge Street became the favored spot for the sea captains to build their sumptuous homes, until at one point nearly every house on the street was owned by a seafarer. Long Wharf, probably the oldest dock in Newport, was built at least as early as 1685 and was the daily scene of frenzied commerce. Ships laden with sugar and molasses from the Indies and dry goods from European ports arrived almost every day. The Newport distilleries and candle-making factories, supplied with whale oil by locally owned whalers, readied their products for export. "Coasters" in turn were loaded from the docks for trade up and down the New England coast. Such was Newport's prowess as a shipping center in the 16th century that a prominent journalist of the day foretold that New York might one day "rival Newport in commercial prosperity and greatness." Here, the merchant princes of the New World, Quakers, Jews and Christians alike, lived in opulent tranquility side by side.

The American Revolution changed all this. The British were especially wary of Newport's prosperity and competition and thus, when hostilities became inevitable, Newport was one of the first places to be occupied. First the British fleet patrolled the harbor and then the troops occupied the town itself. The Point was overrun with soldiers who were quartered in the fine homes without regard to the wishes or privacy of the residents. Other houses and wharf buildings were wantonly destroyed for firewood, and commerce slowly ground to a standstill. After the British were finally routed, the French forces came, and for a brief year, the Point was the scene of courtly splendor and amiable living, but the heyday of commerce was over and was never to be known again.

The houses which remain today have, for the most part, been restored and one can still capture the 18th century atmosphere by simply walking along the narrow streets and letting one's imagination run free.

1. Captain Simeon Potter House
Washington Street

This broad gambrel roof house which actually faces on Marsh Street was built c. 1749. It was the location of Newport's first free school for the poor, set up by the Proprietors of Long Wharf with funds raised by a lottery (an acceptable fund raising practice in those days) and with a sizable donation by Captain Simeon Potter of Bristol, a wealthy privateer. The house and land were also donated by Captain Potter and the school doors opened to 25 students in October, 1814.

2. Edward Gladding House
Washington Street

This two-story, gambrel roof house, built c. 1815, typifies the post-Revolutionary Point dwelling. Constructed by a member of the Gladding family, the house and its neighbors were probably accompanied by stores and wharf buildings on the water side of the street. The Gladdings who were engaged in almost every form of small town enterprise — fishing, boatbuilding, painting, carpentry and store keeping — could be considered a composite early 19th century Point resident.

3. Nancy Murphy House
35 Washington Street

The Murphy House was built as a two-story half house, with gable roof, about 1758. It was a common practice to build a house with the chimney on the end, making it a fairly simple matter to add two rooms on the end of the house, thus creating a central chimney floor plan. The house is also known as the Issac Dayton House as Dayton lived here in the latter part of the 18th century and later went on to found Dayton, Ohio.

4. Brenton Counting House
39 Washington Street

Originally this building stood on Champlin's Wharf at Thames Street opposite Mary Street. It is thought the building dates from the 1740's. The gable roof structure may have originally been built as a house and the gambrel roof structure seems to have been an addition. There is much very fine woodwork and an especially fine stairway. Both Brenton and Champlin were important business houses of the 40's, dealing in extensive foreign trade.

Counting houses were the general business offices for ship owners of the day and this rather imposing building would have well suited the needs of either Brenton or Champlin. Later the building was used as a bank and before road construction forced it to be moved, it continued the tradition of exchange as a pawn shop.

5. Jonathan James House
88 Bridge Street

This high-pitched gambrel roof house was built before 1772. The gambrel roof was a Newport favorite and varied in pitch with the style of the house. Houses were often set with their end to the street to save space.

See map on page 10 for **The Point — Bridge Street**

6. Pitts Head Tavern
77 Bridge Street

The early part of this center chimney, gambrel roof house dates back to 1726 when it was located in the center of town on Washington Square. It was later extensively enlarged and moved twice. It was a very successful 18th century Tavern subsequently used to quarter British and then French forces. It is one of the finest houses on the Point and is an excellent example of the architecture of Newport's early decades. The cream color is an approximation of the original which was discovered during restoration.

7. Christopher Townsend House
74 Bridge Street

This square, gable-on-hip roof house was built c. 1725 by Christopher Townsend, ships cabinetmaker. This was the first of a complex of houses built by the Townsend and Goddard families, whose furniture today is treasured by those fortunate enough to have retained it in their homes here and by museums everywhere.

8. NE corner Second Street

This gambrel roof house was moved to this location in 1969. It originally dates from the 1770's. With its large center chimney and two-room floor plan it is very characteristic of the small 18th century home.

9. Sherman Clarke House
Bridge Street

Mid 18th century, the Clarke House originally stood on Thames Street, end to the
street, on the west side between Pelham and
Green Streets. It was recently moved to this
Bridge Street location when property was
condemned for the new waterfront road.
Records show its existence in 1784. It is typical of the gambrel roof style house so prevalent in Newport.

10. John Townsend House
and Workshop
70-72 Bridge Street

John Townsend, cabinetmaker, owned this
house by 1792. Many details of this gable
roof house with central chimney indicate a
much earlier date, probably before 1740.
The mansard roof building attached to the
west was originally a gambrel roofed workshop for the Townsend cabinetmaking
business. Over the years conversion to living quarters has masked or destroyed all
remnants of 18th century origins. A small
gambrel roofed cottage has been attached to
the east. Very little is known of its history
except that it was moved from Washington
to Marsh Street and recently, to Bridge Street.

11. North Pitman House
59 Bridge Street

Very little detail is known of this gable roof
house. In recent times it was moved to this
location from 28 Farewell Street. The building dates from around 1758. Restoration
gave indications that the building may have
been constructed and first used as a shop or
barn and converted to living quarters at a
later date.

See map on page 10 for **The Point — Bridge Street**

12. 10 Third Street

This two-story, gable roof house is also of mid-18th century origin, but is believed to have been rebuilt after the Revolution. The house itself still faces Third Street, but the gable end, on Bridge Street, has been converted into a shop.

13. The Gardner-Townsend House
53 Bridge Street

Built about 1730, this house was first owned by a William Gardner who sold to Thomas Townsend, one of the many from the Townsend family of cabinetmakers. The house is a fine example of the early smaller gambrel-roofed buildings so popular in Newport.

14. Southwick House
31 Bridge Street

A two story gable roofed house which dates from 1750, it was moved to this location in the 19th century, from Walnut Street. The moving of houses has been a long tradition in Newport as many were moved during the 19th century. This one because the small house on the site became too small. A larger house was found, the smaller moved to the back of the lot and the larger house moved into place. The small house is now a street front location sitting at 23 Bridge Street.

15. Captain Peter Simon House
25 Bridge Street

16. James Gardner House
23 Bridge Street

17. Caleb Claggett House
22 Bridge Street

Built c. 1727, this gable-on-hip roof house was later enlarged to its present size. The original doorway was replaced in the 1800's. The house reflects the fine taste of the sea captains who made their homes along Bridge Street. It is here that Peter Simon, dancing master, brought his Quaker bride, Hannah Robinson, against her father's wishes, only to desert her within a few months.

This little gambrel roof house, built c. 1750, has been moved twice. It is basically a one-story house and has an 18th century lean-to addition.

This brick end, gambrel roof house was built c. 1725. It is interesting to note that despite the brick end, it has a central chimney. The use of brick for any other purpose than a chimney was very rare in Newport at this date. The iron "S" bolts extend through the house and are used to support the masonry walls.

See map on page 10 for **The Point — Bridge Street**

18. William Claggett House
16 Bridge Street

Built a little later than his father's house, this two-story, gable roof house belonged to William Claggett, clockmaker. Some of his clocks are still found in Newport homes, others are in museums. One has ticked daily in the Sabbatarian Meeting House ever since it was presented to the congregation two centuries ago. Claggett also tinkered with electricity and is reputed to have interested Ben Franklin in research on the subject.

19. 3 Bridge Street

This two-story, gable roof house with its two chimneys was probably built in the first half of the 18th century. It has a pedimented doorway and very fine graduated clapboards.

20. Howland House
Bridge Street

The Howland House is a c. 1720 farmhouse which originally stood on the Col. Green estate in Dartmouth, Massachusetts. It was dismantled and recently reconstructed on this site. The angles and pitch of the gambrel roof are more shallow than the typical Newport gambrel. Of note are the sliding dormer type windows.

There is discussion among restorers about moving structures to an area so far from their origin. Instances in Newport seem to arise from the same circumstances — had the building not been dismantled it would have been demolished.

21. Wilder House
53-55 Thames Street

Located originally in Johnston, Rhode Island, the Wilder House was built about 1730 as a large farmhouse. There is evidence of some pre-1700 frame fragments and in its original location indications are that it was used for some time as a tavern or public house.

22. Hathaway House
57 Thames Street

Also known as the Macomber House, this structure was built about 1707 in Assonet, Massachusetts. It has a simple gable roof and was a farmhouse. It is interesting to compare details — windows, trim, doorways, etc. — of this and the previous two buildings all from off island, with the neighboring native Newport buildings.

23. Henry Peckham House
67 Thames Street

The Peckham House has an interesting gable-on-hip roof at the front and a simple gambrel form at the rear. There is a strong dentil molding at the eaves. The delicate fanlight doorway was probably a later addition as construction of the building is believed to be about 1758. Inside is a fine stairway duplicating an original thought to have been made by Townsend.

See map on page 10 for **The Point — Bridge Street**

25. The Jerimiah Lawton House 52 Thames Street

C. 1740. The Lawton House seems to have evolved from a smaller original building to the two chimney central hallway house we see today. It has a very nice pedimented doorway similar to many in the area. The steps and railing seen today date from an earlier period as well.

26. Job Bennett House 44 Thames Street

This broad, gable-on-hip roof house was built in the mid-18th century. During the Revolution it belonged to a Tory who fled Newport when hostilities broke out. To indicate his loyalty to the British, a mark was painted on his chimney, visible from the water. The mark lasted until it was obliterated in 1910 during repairs.

24. Captain William Read House 58 Thames Street

This fine large gambrel roofed house set end to the street probably dates from about 1730. The stairway is original and thought to be another executed by one of the members of the Townsend cabinetmakers.

27. 36 Thames Street

This two-story gambrel roof house, set end to street, was built prior to 1750. It was one of the first on Thames Street to be restored, and with the others to the North, gives a rare glimpse of an 18th century townhouse row.

28. Phillip Stevens House 34 Thames Street

This house with its gable roof and center chimney was built c. 1742. This and others on the street originally belonged to the Stevens family. They were Newport stone-cutters, already established in 1705, and their shop across the street is still in continuous operation, albeit no longer by the Stevens family.

29. John Stevens House 30 Thames Street

This two-story, gable roof house was built in two stages between 1709 and 1750. It may even have undergone another enlargement at a later date. The wide overhung cornice is an indication of its early life.

See map on page 10 for **The Point — Bridge Street**

31. Braman House
18 Thames Street

This two-story, half-house, set with its gable end to the street, was probably built in the late 18th century. It was moved to its present location in the mid-1800's.

30. David Braman Jr. House
26 Thames Street

This two-story, half-house is difficult to date. The framing members exposed during restoration indicate an early building, but the house was not shown on a 19th century survey. It is thought that the original house may have been destroyed during the British occupation and later rebuilt using the remnants of the earlier house.

32. Cozzens House
57-59 Farewell Street

This handsome double house was built c. 1765. It is one of the best examples of the double house built with two separate interior dwellings. The two chimneys each serve one residence. For years this house was in a state of sad disrepair, but has been restored to its original elegance.

33. Common Burying Ground
Corner of Farewell and Warner Streets

Possessing one of the richest collections of fine early stonecarving in New England, the Common Burying Ground is well worth a visit. Among the more than 3,000 stones are the work of the John Stevens family and John Bull, talented Newport stonecarvers.

The Stevens family excelled in fine calligraphy and John Stevens I, II and III all carved for thriving eighteenth century Newport. John III is remembered for his Nathaniel Waldron stone (1769) which reflects a romantic influence. John Bull, a contemporary, produced two spectacular stones. One is a multiple headstone nearly seven feet wide for William Langley's infant children (1785). The other is the Charles Bardin stone (1773) with a figure which may be Bardin himself, Moses or even God.

Worthy of note is an area left of the main body of stones set aside for slaves. These stones are smaller and are charmingly carved.

See map on page 10 for **The Point — Bridge Street**

34. Taggart House
Farewell opposite Warner Street

The Taggart House is an early two story gambrel roofed house, set end to the street. Built c. 1710, it is one of the earlier houses bordering the old Easton Farm. It was originally painted a vibrant blue, one of the early authentic colors recorded for our benefit by 18th century observers. Interesting to note is the fact that recent restoration revealed under layers of shingles patches of plank siding. The material was duplicated and again shows as an interesting alternative to the more common shingles and clapboards.

35. John Stevens Shop
29 Thames Street

This little shop was built by John Stevens in the mid-18th century as a new shop for his marbleworks. The Stevens family had been in business since 1705 and were already known throughout the Colony. The shop has been in continuous operation since that time, and is presently owned by the John Benson family whose skill as stonecutters is nationally known.

36. King's Arms Tavern
6 Cross Street

This square, hip and gable roof house was built in the early 18th century. The massive center chimney is pilastered, common on the larger early chimneys. The house was converted into a tavern in the late 18th century and run successfully as such for many years. It is one of the finest large houses in the Point area.

37. Boss House
9 Cross Street

This center chimney, half-house was built in the first part of the 18th century. It is unrestored and gives an indication of what the majority of the houses on the Point looked like only a few years ago.

38. Governor Gideon Wanton House
11 Cross Street

It is believed that this house was one of the Coddington complex. A date of 1729 is given, but parts of this small two-room center-chimney house may date from the 17th century.

39. Spooner House
1 Elm Street

This two-story, gambrel roof house was built c. 1740. It has the usual central chimney and three room floor plan, very common in this size house.

40. Benjamin Sherburn House
4 Elm Street

Dating from about 1758, this gable roof, central chimney house was moved to this site from Coddington Street when it was slated to be torn down to make way for new buildings. It is a typical mid-18th century house, still retaining a moderately over-hung cornice.

See map on page 10 for **The Point — Bridge Street**

41. Denman House
6 Elm Street

A small central chimney, gable roofed house which was moved from the corner of Charles and North Baptist Streets. The house dates from about 1750. The fanlight doorway dates from the late 18th century.

42. 9 Elm Street

This two-story, gable roof house dates from the very early 18th century. Originally a four room house with a central chimney, it now sports a new addition on the back.

43. Captain Weaver House
14 Elm Street

This two-story, gable roof house originally stood on Bridge Street. It was built c. 1790 and moved to Elm Street towards the end of the 19th century. It has an excellent fanlight door which is original.

44. Third and Elm Street Press
29 Elm Street

The two-story half-house, which forms the basis of this building
was built before 1750. It has been added onto over the years and
finally converted into a shop front. It has a good Greek Revival
cornice. The color of this building resembles the early blue, which
along with barn red and a range of off-whites, was common in the
early 18th century.

45. Samuel Nichols House
31 Elm Street

This gambrel roof house was built c. 1760. Like many other
houses on the Point, it served as a multi-family dwelling for many
years before being restored. The original center chimney and fireplaces are gone, but a house like this and the attractive 19th century houses along this street serves a very important function in
the over-all beautification of the Point.

46. Phillips House
42 Elm Street

This early 18th century half-house with its widely overhung gambrel roof was moved to its present location in the 19th century. The segmental pediment doorway may be the only example of its kind in Newport today.

47. Sheffield-Huntington House
43 Elm Street

This gable roof house was built c. 1719. The wide overhanging cornice is an unmistakable sign of its early date. The house was turned end to the street in the 19th century. The fanlight doorway with the Corinthian detail is not original.

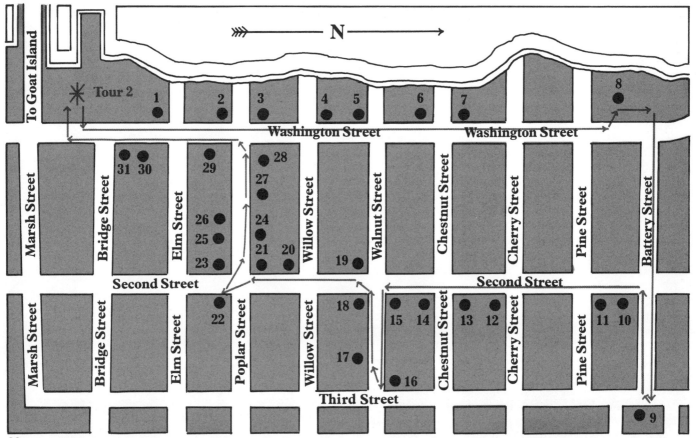

Tour 2
The Point —
Washington Street

The marshy area now known as the Point was the country farm of Governor Nicholas Easton, one of the original settlers of Newport. After he died, his wife sold the farm to the Society of Friends who subdivided it into house lots. Families flocked to the area and by the mid-18th century, the Point was well established. Washington Street, with its big waterside lots, was settled by influential merchants. Wharves extended from Coaster's Island to the Long Wharf. Candlemaking factories were built at the southern end of the Point. Stores were built for the convenience of Point residents. The Proprietors of Long Wharf, incorporated in 1702, were instrumental in providing community services and buildings. The Long Wharf was expanded and kept in repair, a free school was set up, a granary was built (the Brick Market). Often these civic projects were financed by legal lotteries, at other times generous patrons made funds available.

By the outbreak of the Revolution, the Point, in its own right, was an important community. The Revolution created havoc with the commercial interest of the Point. Many merchants, who were Loyalists, fled to other New England towns. The remaining merchants were harassed by the British to the point where they, too, might just as well have fled. The slight recovery in the post-Revolutionary years was annihilated by the War of 1812 and the Point slipped into a gradual decline. While other parts of Newport responded to the impetus of tourism in the 1830's and 40's, the Point decayed. Almost no houses were built during these years.

Now, two hundred years later, the Point has come back to life. The old colonial houses have been rescued and lovingly restored by people from all walks of life. The fine mansions along Washington Street are once again freshly painted and of proud stature. Goat Island will house a hotel and marina. Rose Island has been privately purchased. Parks are being planned in empty lots, some others are slated for colonial houses moved from elsewhere.

Take a minute from this tour to walk down the Elm Street Pier, next to the Hunter House. From this vantage point Washington Street is seen as an entity, as it must have looked to the 18th century seamen pulling up their mooring lines. Looking off in the harbor, one sees Newport today, busy and thriving once again.

1. Hunter House
54 Washington Street

This gambrel roof mansion was built in 1748. It is one of the best examples of colonial American architecture, with its stately shape and excellent trim. William Hunter was our ambassador to Brazil. He became one of Newport's romantic heroes when he married a neighbor, Mary Robinson, outside of her Quaker faith. The house contains a priceless collection of Goddard and Townsend furniture and is open to the public. A Registered National Historic Landmark of the Preservation Society of Newport County.

2. Captain John Warren House
62 Washington Street

This two-story, gambrel roof house was built c. 1736. It was later enlarged. The fanlight doorway may date from this later renovation. The house was used during the Revolution as Headquarters for the French Naval Artillery.

3. Thomas Robinson House
64 Washington Street

The early part of this gambrel roof house probably dates to 1725. In 1760 Quaker Tom Robinson bought it and the hosue remains in the Robinson family today. The furnishings date back to his tenure when he bought them from his neighbor, John Goddard. The house served as the Headquarters for the Vicomte de Noailles who was devoted to the Robinsons ever after.

4. Sanford House
72 Washington Street

This large Victorian house (1870) is one of the few on the Point. It has the typical decorative treatment prominent during the "stick style" period as well as a rather stylized mansard roof. It stands on the site of the John Goddard House before it was moved.

See map on page 30 for **The Point — Washington Street**

5. Captain William Finch House
78 Washington Street

This gambrel roof, center chimney house dates from the mid-18th century. It is exceptional in that it has not undergone any structural changes over the years. At one time it belonged to Captain Thomas Brownell who was sailing master under Oliver Hazard Perry.

6. 86 Washington Street

This Victorian mansion dates from the second half of the 19th century. The many gabled roofline expresses the freely designed interior floor plan. The stucco surface hides the original wood siding, but gives the house the uniform "mass" look common in the mid-19th century.

7. John Tripp House
88 Washington Street

This one-story, gambrel roof cottage dates from the early 18th century. It has a stone end chimney with an ornamented beehive oven. There is only one other known end chimney house in Newport. This one was moved piece by piece from Manton Avenue in Providence and carefully reconstructed by the owners themselves.

8. Battery Park
Washington Street

This park is on the site of the Revolutionary Fort Greene. This fort was built overnight to harass the British ship "Scarborough." The mission was successful for she weighed anchor and fled. It is a marvelous vantage point today for a view of the harbor, Goat Island, the Newport Bridge and the Naval War College on Coaster's Island.

9. Southwick House
77 Third Street

Look ahead to this two-story gable roof house which was built 15 years before the Revolution. It belonged to Solomon Southwick, who was editor and owner of the Newport Mercury prior to the Revolution. He is remembered for his fiery patriotism, summed up in his slogan "Undaunted by tyrants — we'll die or be free!" He buried his press and fled Newport during the British occupation, but later returned.

10. John Goddard House
81 Second Street

This two-story, gambrel roof house was built c. 1750. It has a center chimney with unusual corner fireplaces in each room. The interior trim is exceptional, as one would expect with a Goddard occupant. The Goddards were cabinetmakers who enjoyed a lively business in their day, but could never have known the prices their furniture would bring 200 years later. The block front desk Goddard's design has endured as an unassailable masterpiece.

11. Fairchild Barn
79 Second Street

This barn, built in 1876, is the only remains of an estate on this site. It was built by the architectural firm of McKim, Mead and White who worked widely in Newport. The barn is typical of their work in the 70's — the shingles express the frame and shape of the building and at the same time give it a decorative style, reminiscent of the olde English.

12. John Allan House
67 Second Street

This house with the gable roof and two interior chimneys dates from 1859. The doorway has Greek Revival overtones. The attention devoted to the restoration of a house which is not strictly colonial is an important factor in making the Point a totally attractive living area.

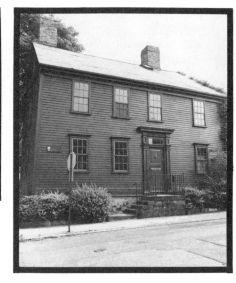

13. George Gibbs House
9 Chestnut Street

This large, gable roof house with two interior chimneys was built c. 1734. It has an excellent doorway, with a dutch door. The outside wall still has the familiar bow that comes with age and has such quaint appeal.

14. 59 Second Street

This gable roof house was on this lot prior to 1758 but was enlarged to its present two-story shape in the 1840's. The Greek Revival details date from the period of this enlargement.

15. Perry House
31 Walnut Street

This broad, two-story gambrel roof house dates from the mid-18th century. It was the birthplace of Matthew Calbraith Perry who is credited with opening the Japan trade. The house had been used as a store and is now being restored.

16. Joseph Wanton House
25 Walnut Street

Earliest established date for the Wanton House seems to be Quaker records of 1770. It is possible this well proportioned gable roofed house was built before this time.

17. Edith Cory House
30 Walnut Street

A date of 1725 is given for this house sometimes known as the Captain James Townsend House. The house was moved from the Northeast corner of Washington and Willow Streets many years ago. Over the years many additions and modifications have been made. At the time of this writing and photograph, restoration was about to commence. It will thus prove interesting to future viewers to compare the above photograph with the research and work that will take place.

18. Solomon Townsend House
51 Second Street

This two-story, gambrel roof house with center chimney was built by Solomon Townsend soon after 1725. The asbestos siding hides a respectable 18th century house.

19. Joseph Belcher House
36 Walnut Street

This one-story, gambrel roof house was built c. 1740. Joseph Belcher was a pewterer, and it is a rare find today to see his initials on the bottom of a piece of pewter. The iron "S" on the chimney is a decorative brace to support the masonry. The pineapple on the post was a common sign of welcome in the 18th century and was often used as an ornament. It was introduced by merchants who brought them back from voyages.

20. James Davis House
42 Second Street

This two-story, gable roof house was built c. 1731. The three-quarter plan, of which it is an example, was common during this period. It is characterized by four windows on the second floor level and three on the first.

21. 57 Poplar Street

This mansard roof house was built c. 1854. The iron balcony railings, denticulated cornice, its freer shape and steep mansard roof all indicate its Victorian origin.

22. John Frye House
31 Second Street

The gambrel roof portion of this house was the original section and dates from 1760. The addition was moved to the site later and used as an ell. The north side still has the original beaded clapboards which were copied when the siding needed replacement.

23. Fowler House
32 Second Street

This two-story, gable roof half-house with its center chimney dates from the mid-18th century. The half-house often served the purpose of a small house which could be enlarged if necessary. Note the three windows across the second story. The fanlight doorway is a common mid-18th century embellishment.

24. 59 Poplar Street

This one-and-a-half story, gambrel roof house was shown on Stiles map (1758). It is set with its end to the street and still has its original chimney. Note the 19th century chimney cap added to prevent downdrafts. There are several houses along this street with chimneys which have been "improved" by one method or another.

25. Chadwick House
54-56 Poplar Street

Two houses have been joined together to form this dwelling. The earlier house was built in the first half of the 18th century, the newer one in 1770. Chadwick was a ship's carpenter who was well known in his time.

26. 58 Poplar Street

This one-and-a-half story, gambrel roof house was probably built c. 1758-76. The little shop attached to the house was on the property first and may have served as a temporary abode while the house was being completed. The chimney is new from the roof.

27. 63 Poplar Street

This gable roof house, set end to the street is a Greek Revival building dating back to 1833. Note the classic temple shape and facade relieved with simple columns. The doorway with its side lights is common on Greek Revival houses.

See map on page 30 for **The Point — Washington Street**

28. John Dennis House
65 Poplar Street

This handsome house was built c. 1740. It has a gambrel roof with a balustrade, central chimney, and excellent pineapple doorway. This doorway is identical to the one on the Hunter House and there is a long tale of door switching to accompany them. The house was moved back from the sidewalk in the late 19th century. At this time, Charles McKim converted the old kitchen into a charming "Queen Anne" living room. He did similar work for the Robinsons across the street.

29. Minturn House
53 Washington Street

This gambrel roof house was built in the mid-18th century. It was moved back from the sidewalk in the 19th century and reoriented with its end to the street. It once belonged to Abraham Riviera, a prominent Jewish merchant. Note the fine fanlight doorway.

30. 43 Washington Street

This gable roof house with two interior chimneys dates from the early 19th century. It has a good Greek Revival doorway with sidelights.

31. George Topham House
41 Washington Street

This two-story, gable roof house built in the mid-18th century was moved here in 1930. It was the home of William Cranston and Joseph Tillinghast, both prominent in the state of Rhode Island.

See map on page 30 for **The Point — Washington Street**

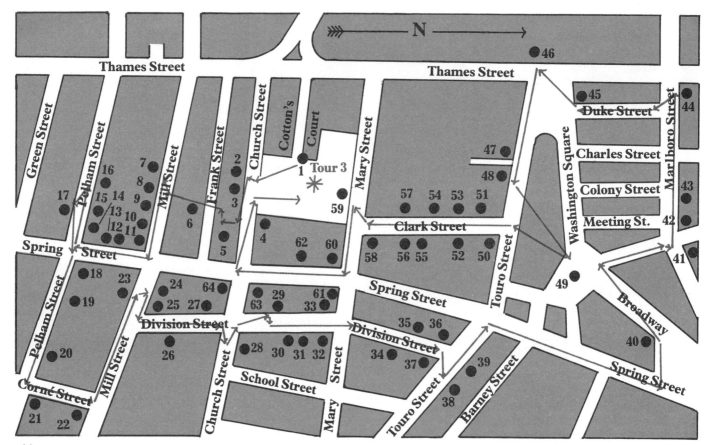

Tour 3
Hill Section

When the first settlers came to Newport in 1639, several men were entrusted with laying out house lots. A long plank walk was laid along the marshy water's edge extending one mile north and south. This street was later made permanent and called Thames Street. House lots extending from the present Spring Street to the Bay were parceled out, each equaling about four acres. The first houses to be built were in the vicinity of the free-flowing spring which originated near the present Colony House. As merchant settlers joined the ranks, houses were built along the hill rising above Thames Street. Here the satisfied landowner could gaze out on the harbor and keep a watch over the activities of his vessels. As time went on, business grew and eventually larger wharves were demanded. One by one these merchants erected warehouses and wharves on the water side of the street until finally the water view was obstructed by their own buildings. Newcomers settled further north on Easton's Point where they too could enjoy close contact with the water. As the city doubled and redoubled in size, tradesmen filled in the remaining house lots with their humble dwellings.

With this rapid surge of growth, the need for various public buildings arose. One of the earliest of these was Trinity Church, designed by Richard Munday. Munday had been living in Newport for several years when he was commissioned to build the church and had undoubtedly impressed his employers with his abilities. He billed himself as a carpenter, but it was obvious that his talents far exceeded those of an ordinary craftsman. With the successful Trinity Church behind him, he went on to build other monuments to his taste. It is thought that he was responsible for the Sabbatarian Meeting House, although there is no documentation to this effect. He was definitely responsible for the Colony House, Newport's first brick building. The Brick Market which stands at the lower end of Washington Square opposing the Colony House, was designed by Peter Harrison twenty years later. Touro Synagogue, also designed by Harrison, rates among the finest buildings of the day.

The Hill and Washington Square reflect a facet of this total development. Most of the early waterfront mansions are gone, all of the 17th century houses which originally stood in the space around the spring have been demolished or drastically changed, and most of the houses which originally faced the open space now known as Washington Square have been torn down or moved. The community of houses which do remain are a living reminder of these early growth years.

1. Dr. Cotton House
4 Cotton's Court

This central chimney, gambrel roof house was built prior to 1758. It still has original exterior woodwork with narrow beaded clapboards. It has a simple but good pedimented doorway. This is the only house remaining on the original Thames Street line.

2. John Langley House
25 Church Street

Records indicate that this central chimney, gable roof, two-story house was built by John Langley c. 1807. It has a good fanlight doorway with interesting trim details. It was moved to this location in 1970.

3. Joseph Wood House
27 Church Street

This two-story, gable roof house was built c. 1810. It has two interior chimneys and a well executed fanlight doorway flanked by Corinthian columns.

4. Erastus Pease House
36 Church Street

The curving gambrel roof on this central chimney house, built in 1785, is very uncommon for this area. It is a style found widely in New York State. The successful effort made by the present owner to adapt this house to its sterile surroundings is worthy of note.

5. Trinity Church
Spring Street

Built in 1725 by Richard Munday, this church is the pride of Newport. It has a simple rectangular plan based on Wren's English examples and although it has been altered, still retains the graceful beauty Munday envisioned. Because of its Anglican affiliations, it was the only church in Newport that was spared abuse by the British occupation. Open to the public, this is a Registered National Historic Landmark.

See map on page 44 for **Hill Section**

6. Honeyman Hall
Frank Street

This Greek Revival building was named in honor of the Reverend James Honeyman, rector of Trinity Church. The hall was designed to harmonize with the park setting off Newport's landmark Church.

7. Mill Street

Built in 1885-6, this brick firehouse was home for Steam Fire Company #1 until 1913. Through this period small firehouses, seven in all, served Newport. In 1913 centralization and mechanization forced abandonment of many of these buildings. Rarely does such attention to design find a place in the municipal buildings of today.

An exemplary instance of modern use within an existing framework, the firehouse is now a shop complete with brass pole.

8. Coggeshall House
Mill Street

A unique double house which was built about 1784, this is a long two-story gable roofed dwelling with two interior chimneys. One chimney serves each interior house. Also interesting is the passageway to the rear courtyard which is indicative of the tightness of lot size in the crowded early city of Newport. The house was recently moved to this location for restoration.

9. Beriah Brown House
41 Mill Street

A large farmhouse which originally stood in North Kingston, Rhode Island, the Beriah Brown House was disassembled several years ago and is now being reconstructed at this location. Parts of the frame date from the very early 1700's. Additions over the years give it the large gambrel roof structure we can see today. Many rooms have very fine detail in the interior woodwork.

See map on page 44 for **Hill Section**

10. Joseph Beattie House
47 Mill Street

This two-story, gambrel roof house was built prior to 1758. Although the exterior has been covered with asbestos shingles and the doorway removed, it still retains its fine early lines and central chimney.

11. Alexander Jack Jr. House
Corner Mill and Spring Streets

This two-story, gable roof house is a typical three-quarter house. Records indicate that it was built in 1811, but some interior details suggest an earlier date. The three-quarter plan reoccurs frequently in Newport houses built toward the end of the 18th century. The fanlight doorway is particularly good.

12. Samuel Bours House
175 Spring Street

A large two-story gambrel roofed building of the half house floor plan arrangement, the Bours House was probably built before 1777. It is typical of many end to the street houses in Newport. The pedimented front doorway is very typical and elegant in its simplicity.

13. Jonathan Gibbs House
181 Spring Street

Built by Jonathan Gibbs, a housewright, sometime before 1777, this is typical of the tiny two-room gambrel roof cottage style of structure often seen in Newport. This one with its end to the street was always squeezed for land, probably the reason it never acquired the lean-to addition across the near wall similar to the Gardner House at 23 Bridge Street, or the Belcher House at 36 Walnut Street.

14. Daniel Vaughn House
50 Pelham Street

This gable roof, two-story house was built c. 1760. With its center chimney it is a typical house of the period. It has undergone extensive remodeling, however, especially apparent in the Greek Revival trim and later Victorian changes to the roof line.

15. Daniel Vaughn House
44 Pelham Street

In 1781 this land was confiscated from Thomas Bannister. Vaughan, who owned the building next door at 50 Pelham, bought the land in 1785. It is probable that this large gambrel roof house was built about 1800. It is of the central hall, two interior chimney floor plan.

See map on page 44 for **Hill Section**

18. John Bannister House
56 Pelham Street

This broad, gambrel roof house was built c. 1751. It has two interior chimneys and the central hall plan. This was one of many houses and buildings owned by Bannister, a prominent merchant and smuggler. The recessed doorway may have been the result of General Prescott's occupation of the house during the Revolution.

16. Dr. David King House
32 Pelham Street

This large gambrel roof house was built c. 1710. The two interior chimneys indicate a central hall interior plan. It has several 18th century additions and is being restored. The doorway was once removed and was recently discovered and returned to its original place.

17. Lucina Langley House
43 Pelham Street

This one-story, gambrel roof house was built c. 1771. The two room central chimney floor plan was frequently used throughout the 18th century in Newport. Many of these houses had lean-to additions which give them the familiar "salt-box" roof line.

19. Augustus Littlefield House
70 Pelham Street

This Greek Revival house was built in 1836 for Littlefield. It is patterned after an Italian "villa" seen by Littlefield on one of his voyages. Although it retains the traditional Greek temple outline, the heavy cornice gives away the Italian influence.

20. 80 Pelham Street

Built during the mid-19th century, this small mansard roof shingle house exhibits a wide variety of decorative trim elements. Note the bracketed cornice, extensive window detail and wood rope molding on the roof corners.

21. 92 Pelham Street

Like its neighbor to the west, this larger house was also of a mid-19th century date. The design is typical of the freedom indulged in with the advent of balloon framing. Trim elements run the whole range of stylistic periods.

22. Michel Felice Corné House
2 Corne Street

This two-story, gable roof house was built after the turn of the century. It has a nice fanlight doorway and a large ell addition. Corné was an Italian mural painter who achieved great renown for his seascapes. He is well known in Newport for his Great Lake battle scenes.

23. J. T. O'Connell Mill
75 Mill Street

This brick building dates from the 19th century. An effort was put into design and construction of commercial buildings in this era. This mill, still in operation, bears testimony to their durability.

24. 62 Mill Street

This two-story, gable roof house was built c. 1807. The broad roof indicates an advanced floor plan, providing more comfortable living space. It is in the process of restoration, but for many years lay hidden under asbestos siding.

25. Billy Bottomore House
70 Mill Street

This two-story, gable roof house was built in the early 18th century. It has a center chimney with a large keeping room fireplace, indicating its early date. It has been carefully restored to keep the original floor plan intact.

26. 80 Division Street

This square, hip roof house was built between 1750 and 1760. It is a style much in vogue in Newport during this period, with interior chimneys and rooms in each corner. The house has had numerous additions and some changes over the years.

27. William Card House
73 Division Street

This two-story, gable roof house was built in 1811. It is again a three-quarter house, common in this period, with one window on one side of the door and four instead of five across the second story. It has a lovely old-fashioned garden which can be glimpsed from the sidewalk.

See map on page 44 for **Hill Section**

28. Thomas Goddard House
78 Church Street

This house was built by Thomas Goddard c. 1800. It is a two-story, gable roof house with rusticated window caps. It has excellent interior detail reflecting the abilities of its first owner.

29. 49 Division Street

This 19th century church has been completely remodeled as an artist's studio and residence. Only its exterior gives away its original purpose.

30. Dr. Samuel Hopkins House
46 Division Street

This two-story gambrel roof house was built c. 1751. It is set with its end to the street. The Reverend Hopkins who lived here 1770-1805 was the hero of one of Harriet Beecher Stowe's novels.

31. Ailman House
42 Division Street

Built about 1748, the Ailman House is a simple central chimney half house floor plan with a pretty, simple pedimented doorway on the north end of the facade. The gable roof ends at the eaves in a fairly wide overhang typical of many earlier simple houses.

32. Augustus Lucas House
40 Division Street

This square, hip roof house was built c. 1721. It was enlarged toward the end of the 18th century. This may account for the fact that the two interior chimneys are oriented in front and back instead of to the side as would be the case in an original hip-roof house. It has an excellent pedimented doorway.

33. Nassau Hastie House
37 Division Street

This large, two-story, gambrel roof house belonged to Nassau Hastie, a barber, and was probably built by him shortly after he bought the land in 1760. It has a good pedimented doorway.

34. Daniel Carr House
20 Division Street

An early house, dating from about 1712, this is another two-story house with a steeply pitched gable roof with a rather wide overhang at the cornice line. Evidence indicates a chimney at one end, and this with several other features tends to verify the early date of this simple house.

35. Elisha Gibbs House
5 Division Street

This small, gable roof house was built c. 1745. It has a wide overhanging cornice, usually found on earlier houses, but is none-the-less typical of mid-18th century Newport.

36. Rhodes-Tillinghast House
3 Division Street

Also known as the Tanner House, this gable roof building seems to have been built by Samuel Rhodes about 1714. It is typical with a half house floor plan and an attractive fan-light doorway, probably added in the late 18th century.

37. Levi Gale House
Touro Street

This unusual Greek Revival house was built c. 1835. Instead of following the usual lines of the Greek temple, it is a square, flat-roofed house. The Grecian influence is carried out with the pilasters on its facade and with the entry columns. The siding, as was usual, is horizontal sheathing. It was moved to its present site in 1915.

38. Newport Historical Society (Sabbatarian Meeting House)
82 Touro Street

The little Meeting House attached to the rear of the Historical Society resembles Munday's work in Trinity Church and is frequently attributed to him. It was built in 1729 and has been moved twice. The interior is well worth seeing. As well as the Claggett clock which hangs in the Meeting House, the Historical Society houses a fine collection of Newport furniture and other Newport material and is open to the public.

See map on page 44 for **Hill Section**

39. Touro Synagogue
72 Touro Street

This was Peter Harrison's third public building in Newport, dedicated in 1763. It took four years to complete and is considered his masterpiece. The austere exterior, oriented at an angle to the street to comply with Jewish ritual, cloaks one of the finest interiors in the country. Open to the public, this is a Registered National Historic Landmark.

40. Wanton-Lyman-Hazard House
17 Broadway

Built probably just before 1700 by Stephen Munford, the Hazard House is a gem of 17th century architecture. It has a large central chimney and two rooms on either side. The steeply pitched roof has an interesting kick at the eaves to incorporate the huge rounded plaster cove — all of this seems to be original to the house. The facade and doorway we see today are very likely 18th century "modernizations." The interior remains a very simple blend of 17th and 18th century elegance. The house is open to the public.

41. The Quaker Meeting House
Farewell Street

The Quakers had a very early and long lasting influence in Newport. The original hip-roof turreted meeting house was built in 1700. The building as seen today is the result of major enlargements in the early 19th century, necessary to accommodate ever increasing numbers of Friends. The building has been recently restored, revealing much of the original framework inside. The Meeting House is open to the public.

42. Whitehorse Tavern
Farewell at Marlboro

One of Newport's earliest buildings, a two-room, two story house with a huge pilastered chimney, was probably constructed by 1673. The Whitehorse is thought to be the oldest tavern in the country, William Mayes Sr. having a license to sell "all sorts of Strong Drink" in 1687. In the 18th century the tavern kept by Jonathan Nicholls II, who owned the Hunter House. Prominent and popular throughout its history, the Whitehorse appears today in enlarged 18th century form. It is today, as it was 300 years ago, a fine tavern and restaurant.

See map on page 44 for **Hill Section**

43. St. Paul's Methodist Church
Marlboro Street

Built in 1806, St. Paul's is a fine example of 19th century church architecture. Typical of parish church design, it has its tower at the entrance. This building has been raised to allow basement space.

44. Coddington House
2 Marlboro Street

For many years the Governor John Coddington House rested one story off the street, to accommodate a large store at ground level. Recent restoration removed the store and lowered the house (c. 1730) to street level. John Stevens carved a shell hooded doorway for this house about 1737. The original was lost but Stevens followed the lines put down by Richard Munday in his plans for the Ayrault House. The Ayrault House is gone, but its doorway survives and the present one on the Coddington House was drawn from it.

45. Newport National Bank
Abraham Roderiques Riviera House
Washington Square

This large, gambrel roof building was built in the first half of the 18th century and enlarged before 1758. In 1803 it became the Bank headquarters, facing on the newly laid out Mall. In 1950 it was very carefully restored. It is an excellent example of a colonial building adapted to commercial use without destroying its integrity.

46. The Brick Market
127 Thames Street

The Proprietors of Long Wharf planned and financed this fine market building. It was designed by Peter Harrison and finally completed, after eleven years, in 1772. Like Munday's Colony House, this building was also drawn from English sources. Brick was used for each, a departure from normal building practice in Newport. It is to both men's credit that they were each able to produce a building with such a distinct colonial air. A Registered National Historic Landmark open to the public.

47. Peter Buliod House
29 Touro Street

The Buliod House was built about 1755 as a large three-story mansion befitting its Mall location . It has a shallow hip roof with detailed cornices and formal rusticated siding. The house has been the Rhode Island Bank, billet for French troops, and a home for the Salvation Army. The Buliod House, is under restoration by the Newport Restoration Foundation, and will incorporate panelling and a stairway from the destroyed Jahleel Brenton Mansion.

See map on page 44 for **Hill Section**

48. Joseph and Robert Rogers House
37 Touro Street

This three-story, hip roof house was built c. 1798 and is a good example of the transition to Federal style houses. The fanlight doorway is particularly sophisticated with its Corinthian columns. It now serves as headquarters for the Newport Preservation Society.

49. Colony House
Washington Square

Richard Munday designed this brick assembly house which was built in 1739. Munday was also responsible for several other buildings in Newport, notably the beautiful Trinity Church. Although he claimed to be only a builder, he was well acquainted with English architecture and this excellent building, surmounted by a cupola and balustrade, once again serves as a reminder that Newport enjoys a rich heritage of fine buildings. A Registered National Historic Landmark.

50. Wilbur-Ellery House
51 Touro Street

Over the years this house suffered many changes. It is now under restoration and will be returned to the three-story hip roofed mansion house typical of its c. 1800 date. In 1809 William Ellery III, son of the signer of the Declaration of Independence, owned the house and lived here for many years.

51. The Bell House
11 Clarke Street

This house has been extensively altered. It was originally a two-story, gable roof house of the mid-18th century period. It was raised to its present level to make room for a lower level garage. It presently houses a silversmith shop.

52. Ezra Stiles House
14 Clarke Street

This two-story, gambrel roof house was built c. 1756 as a parsonage for the Second Congregational Church opposite. This is where Ezra Stiles lived when he was minister of the church (1775-76). He is remembered for his careful survey and map of Newport in 1758, and was one of the most-learned scholars ever to sojourn in our city. When the Revolution disrupted church services, he left Newport to become president of Yale College.

See map on page 44 for **Hill Section**

54. The Newport Artillery
23 Clarke Street

This handsome stone armory was originally built in 1835 by Alexander McGregor, the Scottish stonemason responsible for Fort Adams. The Newport Artillery is now the oldest active military organization in the United States. Open to the public.

53. 2nd Congregational Church
Clarke Street

This church was built by Cotton Palmer in 1735. It has undergone extensive changes which account for the Greek Revival and Victorian touches. It has not been used as a church for many years, and efforts are being made to save it and restore it to its original condition.

55. Joseph Burrill House
28 Clarke Street

This steep, gambrel roof house dates from the early 18th century. The interior suggests that the house was extensively enlarged, accounting for its unusual height. The doorway is later.

56. Simon Pease House
32 Clarke Street

Recent restoration of the Pease House has revealed an early 17th century frame. Under years of modifications and additions, a simple two room two-story house with a huge chimney was detailed. The steeply pitched roof timbers showed strong evidence for the kick at the eaves similar to, though less grand than, the one original to the Wanton-Lyman-Hazard House.

57. Robert Stevens House
31 Clarke Street

This gambrel roof house set with its end to the street dates from the early 18th century. It has a good fanlight doorway probably added at a later date. It was used during the Revolution to quarter French troops.

58. Vernon House
Clarke Street

Although the original part of this house dates from the early 18th century, the house as it stands today was probably enlarged by Metcalf Bowler in 1759. He was a wealthy merchant who already owned a country estate, and he spared no expense in renovating this house. The rusticated exterior has been attributed to Peter Harrison. During the Revolution, this house was used as Commander Rochambeau's headquarters. Registered National Historic Landmark.

See map on page 44 for **Hill Section**

59. Christopher Fowler House 29 Mary Street

The Fowler House is a large two-story gambrel roofed building with two interior chimneys. It was built about 1801 on a traditional central hallway, room in each corner, floor plan. The fanlight doorway has excellent delicate detailing.

60. Jonathan Otis House 109-111 Spring Street

Otis, a goldsmith, was the owner of record in 1777, but the house probably dates from an earlier period. It is thought to have been built by John Odlin in the early 18th century, c. 1705. The original house seems to have been of the two-story one room plan with a large chimney end. Early additions formed another room with a brick end. It is under restoration now after extensive changes over the years.

61. 104-08 Spring Street

This two-story, gable roof house appears on Stiles map (1758). It has been altered to house a shop and is one of many old houses along Spring Street which have undergone commercial modernization.

63. Borden House
134–36 Spring Street

This two-story, gambrel roof house was built in the first half of the 18th century. It has two interior chimneys and has been converted into a shop.

64. Naval and Underseas Museum
138 Spring Street

Many treasures, artifacts, and relics of the sea are to be seen in this small museum. Most of the displays have been found in waters off the Eastern U.S. coast and in the Caribbean Sea. Open to the public.

62. Samuel Barker House
119 Spring Street

This two-story, gambrel roof house dates back to c. 1714. It is one of the few brick end houses in Newport, as brick was rarely used except in chimney construction. It has four end chimneys and a good fanlight doorway.

See map on page 44 for **Hill Section**

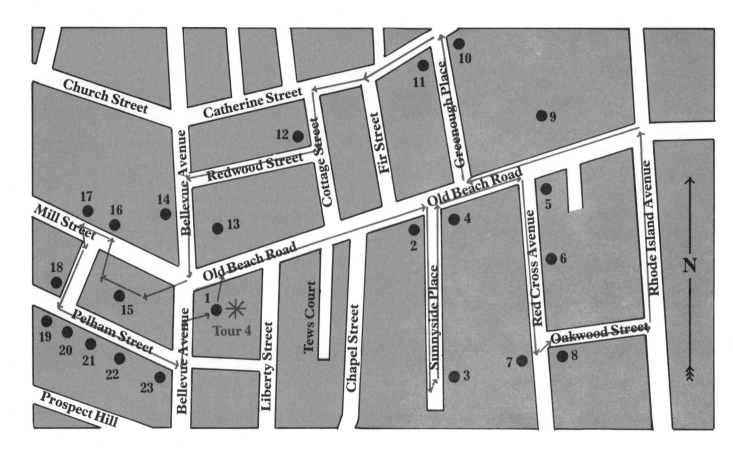

Church Street

Catherine Street

Bellevue Avenue

Redwood Street

12

Cottage Street

Fir Street

Greenough Place

10

11

9

17

16

14

Mill Street

13

Old Beach Road

Old Beach Road

5

4

2

18

15

1

Tour 4

Liberty Street

Tews Court

Chapel Street

Sunnyside Place

3

Red Cross Avenue

6

Rhode Island Avenue

N

Pelham Street

Bellevue Avenue

Oakwood Street

8

19

20

21

22

23

7

Prospect Hill

Tour 4
Redwood Library Area

This is an unusual tour because in this one small area there is as rare a collection of houses as anywhere in America. During the 19th century when architecture was coming into its own, there were a handful of men who were responsible for defining the style of Victorian houses and, although they were widely known elsewhere, were all setting this style in Newport. In addition, the first man to be recognized as an architect in America, Peter Harrison, designed an extraordinary building here, the first of its kind on this continent, which eventually had a profound influence on our national style. He based his Redwood Library drawings on what he considered an appropriate Palladian model. It was his first experience with a large building and he borrowed freely. It was a tremendous success. He went on to design other buildings in Newport, notably the Brick Market and the Touro Synagogue, but his reputation was already established. The Redwood Library was his proving ground.

It was this same mood of experimentation which prevailed more than a century later in this same area. Charles McKim, William Mead and Stanford White, newly associated in their New York firm when they were working within these blocks, are generally considered to be the deans of 19th century American architecture. Mead, the quiet member of the firm, was more than offset by the creative energies of his two partners, but it was he who was chiefly responsible for the persistent return to the European influence in their work. McKim provided the disciplined simplicity inherent in their work, and White, the flair for decoration. (An unmistakable sign of White's handiwork is the brightly colored mosaic which he fashioned out of broken glass or shells and set into the shingled surface of his houses.) Richard Morris Hunt, best known for his elegant mansions built for the Vanderbilts, also went through the throes of defining his style during his early period. There are two important wooden houses on this tour which show this side of Hunt's work. The Griswold House was a very clear statement of the "stick style" so popular in the 1860's and 70's. The other, the Colonel Waring House, he built for himself and is a complete departure from his work elsewhere. He was exploring new avenues with wood, and the resulting house has often been called the precursor of the Colonial Revival house.

George Champlin Mason, the author of **Newport and Its Cottages** (1875) may have been the first architectural spokesman who was able to foretell the trend in Victorian architecture. He also designed and built a house for himself in this area. In this case, the house does not look ahead to the future so much as it sums up the whole mood of the Victorian return to natural and comfortable living quarters. The house is a melange of a number of styles, the Swiss chalet or rustic European model, "carpenter Gothic," expressed in the trim and purely American, "stick style" in the treatment of the siding, and a foretaste of the half-timber medieval look which was to appear in full force ten years later.

1. The Art Association
76 Bellevue Avenue

This house, also known as the Griswold House, was built in 1862. It was designed by Richard Morris Hunt and is one of his best "stick style" efforts. The framing members of the house are expressed in the finished product as something worthy of notice. To accomplish this effect, Hunt used diagonal and vertical "sticks" to off-set the open spaces and voids on its surface. This counterplay of textures against the skeleton of the house is the one unfailing sign of a "stick style" house. Open to the public.

2. Commodore
William Edgar House
29 Old Beach Road

This large brick mansion was designed by McKim, Mead and White in 1885-86. It reflects the progression from their pure Colonial Revival mood to their own adaptation of the same, resulting in a house which resembles a Tudor manor with a style of its own.

3. Samuel Tilton House
Sunnyside Place

This house was also designed by McKim, Mead and White in 1881-82. It shows more originality than the Edgar House and is a good example of their early shingle work. Note the interesting chimneys and the use of windows to break up the monotony of the surface. The bits of glass imbedded in the plaster panel was Stanford White's own special decorative touch.

4. George
Champlin Mason House
31 Old Beach Road

This house was Mason's own creation built
in 1873. While McKim, Mead and White
were responsible for most "shingle style"
work of merit in Newport, Mason could be
called the champion of the movement. He,
with A. J. Downing, articulated the basics of
building a "villa" and wrote on the subject.
Here he combined the basic chalet shape, the
English half-timber look and highly ornamented trim unique to 19th century America.

5. Katherine Prescott Wormeley
House
2 Red Cross Avenue
(SW corner Old Beach Road)

This McKim, Mead and White house was
built 1876-77. It has elements of the Tudor
influence, although it remains refreshingly
American. The architects have not refined
their "shingle style" efforts here to the
same point as in others in this area.

6. Skinner House
6 Red Cross Avenue

Another McKim, Mead and White house,
this one was built in 1882. It is on a smaller
scale than most of their houses but retains
the familiar tower, shingle work and varied
exterior shape.

See map on page 70 for **Redwood Library Area**

7. Samuel Coleman House
7 Red Cross Avenue

This house was built in 1882-83 by McKim, Mead and White. It is the same basic "shingle style" as the others in this area, but its simple gambrel roof with dormers is somewhat unusual for this firm. It seems to be in their Colonial Revival spirit based perhaps on American rather than English examples. The piazza, plaster panel and shinglework are typical.

8. Cor. Oakwood Terrace
and Red Cross Avenue

This Colonial Revival mansion is typical of the latter half of the 19th century. The pebblestone surface is unusual, but the treatment of the windows and cornice is Palladian, as is the doorway flanked with huge Corinthian columns.

9. Belair
Old Beach Road opp.
Red Cross Avenue

This mansard roof house was built in 1870 and is in the Tuscan revival style. The gatekeeper's house and stable in this same design have been preserved and can still be seen from the road.

10. Colonel George Waring House
33 Greenough Place

Richard Morris Hunt built this house for himself in 1870-71. While the date is a little early for strict Colonial Revival architecture, this little house has a distinct colonial simplicity about it. Note in particular the gambrel and hip roof which is quite a departure from the steep Gothic gables still very current. The trim details, especially over the doorway, hark back to the rustic Swiss chalet look.

11. Clement C. Moore House
35 Catherine Street

This house, built c. 1850, is a rambling Victorian house. Its special significance is that Clement C. Moore who wrote the immortal "Night Before Christmas" in 1823 lived here several years. This is just one more instance of Newport's attraction to men of letters.

12. Redwood Street (NW corner Cottage Street)

This Gothic style "cottage" was built in 1846. With its cruciform shape, high gables and sheathed exterior, it represents the normal small Victorian house built throughout Newport. Its original lines have been somewhat obscured by alterations.

See map on page 70 for **Redwood Library Area**

13. Redwood Library
Bellevue Avenue

This exceptionally fine 18th century building was designed by Peter Harrison, "America's first architect." In keeping with the times it is built of wood, but reflects Harrison's knowledge of classic architecture to the fullest degree. The wood is rusticated and sanded to resemble stone, the trim is, in every case, the purest Palladian style. The net effect is that of a simple Roman temple. This building, for which Harrison was never paid, was to have a profound influence on the budding science of architecture in America.

14. Samuel Pratt House
49 Bellevue Avenue

The Pratt House, built in 1871, has many similarities to the Waring House (# 11 on this tour). There is no direct evidence that Richard Morris Hunt designed this building, but many of the design elements are very much his style, as well as being indicative of the stick style in general. Of interest in this small house is the use of colored slate siding and the various trim features. Surely the towers in a house of this size would have been of little practical use and therefore must be considered stylistic devices.

15. Touro Park

This little park in the center of town, houses the subject of one of the wordiest disputes in the history of architecture. The Stone Mill, which stands 84 feet above sea level, was once thought to be a relic from the days of Norse exploration. A favorite 19th century explanation was that it was Governor Benedict Arnold's "stone mill." A recent thesis entertains the possibility of Portuguese construction during early explorations in the New World. The origin of the structure still remains open to speculation.

See map on page 70 for **Redwood Library Area**

16. Charles Sherman House
128 Mill Street

This excellent example of Greek Revival architecture was built prior to 1850. It is set, as usual, with its end to the street although the entrance is on the side. The trim is all in the Doric order, and the sheathing is horizontal, but no longer clapboarded.

17. Robert Lawton House
118 Mill Street

This three-story, hip roof house was built in 1809. It is one of the very few Federal period houses built in Newport and is a nice example of the style. The paucity of Federal style houses in Newport can be readily understood when one recalls the post-Revolutionary war depression that was especially severe here.

18. 5 Touro Park West

This stately mansion with hip roof reflects the competing elements in early Victorian architecture. It has traces of the Federal period in the doorway. Greek Revival trim and Palladian details.

19. Swinburne House 115 Pelham Street

This is another pre-1850 Greek Revival house with a characteristic entrance supported by Ionic columns. The horizontal sheathing terminates in fine rusticated corner trim. The house is a fine example of the period. It presently serves as a school of household arts.

20. White House 123 Pelham Street

This Greek Revival house is similar to its neighbor, but is slightly more formal. Note the railing which surrounds the porch entry and planked facade with columns supporting the wide frieze below the roof.

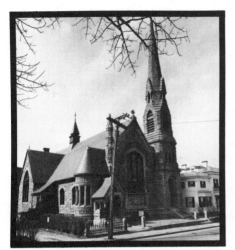

21. Channing Memorial Church
Pelham Street

This rough-cut stone church was completed in 1881 and was named in memory of William Ellery Channing. He was born in Newport in 1780 and was the first Unitarian-Congregationalist minister, as well as a spokesman for his times.

22. 135 Pelham Street

This arch-Victorian house is typical of large frame houses built in the second half of the 19th century by carpenters working from standard plans. The trim was often very elaborate, only possible after the advent of band saws.

23. The Elk's Home
141 Pelham Street

To avoid capture by the Confederate troops during the Civil War, the U.S. Naval Academy was transferred to the Atlantic House Hotel on this site. The hotel was subsequently demolished and replaced by this rambling Victorian house built in 1877 by Seth B. Stitt.

See map on page 70 for **Redwood Library Area**

General Introduction
Bellevue Avenue Area

Newport, the commercial center of 18th century America, was to become the vacation resort of the 19th century. As early as 1729 Newport was already known among the English settlers in the West Indies as a watering place akin to home. By mid-century, wealthy plantation owners had already made it a custom to send their wives and families to Newport for the summer months to escape the scorching heat. During the long post-war recovery period, when Newport was struggling to refresh her resources, this attractiveness to tourists helped to save the day. After the War of 1812, tourism began to show a marked increase. Hotels and boardinghouses sprung up to accommodate the influx of summer visitors. It wasn't until around 1844, when the first Ocean House Hotel was built, that the summer colony began to flower in its own right in Newport. By 1852 twelve summer residences had been built, most of them extending along the farm lands from Touro Street southward (the present Bellevue Avenue). Newport was again on the verge of a new era of prosperity, this time generated by wealth earned elsewhere and distilled in the fine buildings which were soon to crop up all along the southern tip of the island.

It isn't entirely coincidental that this emergence of Newport as a summer colony came about during the same period that architecture was coming into its own professionally. The early homes of Colonial America were built by craftsmen adept at making a practical dwelling. Now, there was to be a trend toward expressing the taste and wealth of the homeowner in the house he built. Architects, still considered draftsmen in the age of Munday and Harrison, were now all schooled in the classic elements of architecture, and felt free to expand upon this knowledge. The availability of money and materials, especially in Newport, gave them an opportunity to vent their ideas. Newport was the scene of many architectural innovations, after which houses all over the country were later patterned. For the first time, interiors were the subject of special attention to every detail and an elite corps of interior decorators developed. The setting and grounds of these houses were also given scrupulous thought and were often planned by landscape architects. There was an aura of professionalism about these buildings which was new in America.

For the most part, the houses one sees on this tour fall into three categories. The first, following on the heels of Greek Revival architecture, was an expressive return to nature. Sometimes loosely termed Gothic, this period coincided with the 19th century romanticism rampant in the arts. Roof lines were freed from the strictures of the Colonial and Greek Revival periods, windows, doors anf porches began to appear in relation to the changing interior rather than on a set exterior plan. The house took on the form of its surroundings and reflected its rural setting. This concern with nature and reality showed itself in new treatments of the exterior of the house itself. Instead of covering the house with clapboards or shingles, the house was boarded vertically, with ornamental "sticks" indicating the structural members of the frame. Symmetry and beauty were synonymous. In the stone buildings of this period, there was an effort to produce this symmetry by having a uniform surface. A lot of the inventiveness which characterized their wooden neighbors was lost in these first stone buildings, but it was this form of the Gothic mood which took precedence in the early mansions or "villas" of Newport. It is not at all uncommon to see a wooden house, either built to resemble masonry, or stuccoed over for the same effect. It was the early experiments with expressive use of wood, though, commonly referred to as "stick style," which was to have the most enduring influence on the summer colony architecture. It eventually led into the development of a new style in the 1870's, known as the Queen Anne or Tudor revival. This period, in its prime, saw the emergence of a stylistic half-timbered house in the old English tradition. The bottom half of masonry, the top of shingles or slate, the houses had a medieval look about them. Within, the rooms expressed the comfort and rich warmth of the colonial home, on a grander scale. The vertical look of the Gothic era gave way to a more compact horizontal house. Shingles were used as a decorative medium much as the battens or "sticks" had been used in prior decades (thus the term "shingle style" which is sometimes used to define the houses of this period). This type of architecture was to see its full development in Newport before giving way to the monumental architecture of the late 19th century which falls into a class by itself. Architects were now banded together in a professional sense, schools were founded, treatises published. The profession was still young in America though, and most of our architects were educated abroad. Academic ideas began to exert themselves in the buildings of these architects. Buildings became more abstract, less related to function or surroundings. In Newport, the industrial magnates of the late 19th century employed these architects to construct their mansions. The houses became the embodiment of their wealth, showing an increasing tendency toward grandeur for the sake of display. There are several examples of this eclectic architecture in Newport, the Breakers being perhaps the most sumptuous and palatial of them all.

Three separate tours follow. The first, unless one is exceptionally stalwart, is a driving tour. It extends from Bellevue Avenue southward around the famed Ocean Drive. There is an example of virtually every style house from the Swiss chalet, whcih formed the basis for the early "stick style" houses, to the 20th century copies of European chateaux so numerous on the ocean edge. The second and third tours merely expand the scope of this first tour by giving one a closer glimpse on foot. In all three tours there are numerous houses which are not mentioned per se, but they should also be appreciated as part of a unique summer colony environment unparalleled anywhere.

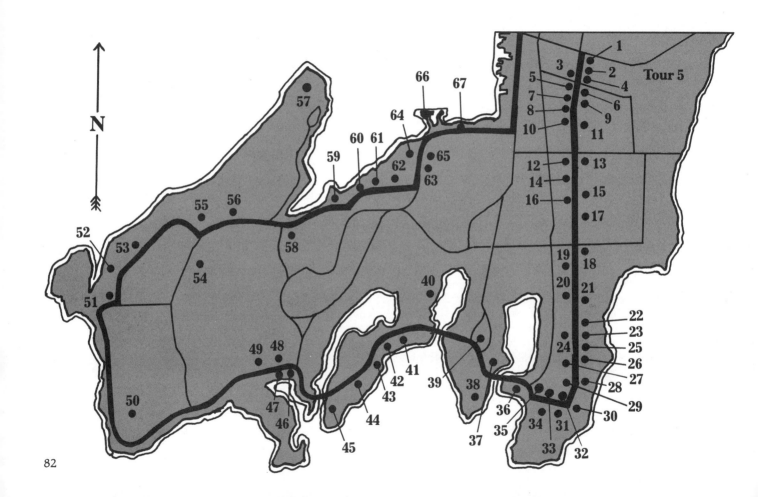

N

Tour 5

Tour 5
Bellevue Avenue — Ocean Drive

Bellevue Avenue only a little over a century ago was a dusty lane leading out from town. In the few short years after 1850 when Newport "cottages" were proliferating madly on both sides of the Avenue, it was transformed into the most important three mile stretch in the social annals of America. During this era there was no modesty about wealth—it was to be enjoyed and displayed. Faces were to be seen, names to be dropped. Parties, teas and balls were planned with utmost attention to every detail. Sporting events were eagerly anticipated and supported. Intellectual pursuits were varied and wide-ranged. In short, Bellevue Avenue supported a bustle of activity unique to its location. Aside from the routine travel on one's daily course of affairs, the Avenue was the scene of the daily drive at sunset when the equipages were spangled in all their finery, and driven up and down the two lane road. Perhaps the finest array was that of the Belmonts, whose stable of horses were reputed to have three sets of tack—for morning, afternoon and evening use. When Ocean Drive was completed, the driving custom was carried on, although the mode of transportation slowly changed from the horse-drawn vehicle to the motor car.

This Drive, which snakes along the water's edge from Bailey's Beach to Castle Hill, is a marvel of beauty. Lined with wild rosa rugosa hedgerows, marshes filled with waving cat-tails and offset by the sparkle of the open sea, it is the natural setting for the fine manor houses built here after the turn of the century. This area was almost totally unexploited prior to the summer colony invasion, although traces of early 17th and 18th century farms can be glimpsed here and there. Nearly the whole tip of the island from Almy Pond to Fort Adams once belonged to William Brenton (d. 1674) after whom Brenton's Point is named. His farm was extensive and sophisticated, befitting an early settler of means.

It is difficult to take in so much splendor and natural beauty in one short drive, and one always feels compelled to return to these unspoiled assets of the "isle of peace."

1. Travers Block
Bellevue Avenue (E)

Built c. 1875 by Richard Morris Hunt as shops with bachelor quarters, this block has a definite medieval air, and although it is not an exceptional example, shows the use of half-timber construction prevalent at the time.

2. The Casino
Bellevue Avenue (E)

Built between 1879 and 1881, the Newport Casino is one of the best "shingle style" buildings in Newport. It was built by the architectural firm of McKim, Mead and White and was one of the first "country clubs" on the East Coast. It is open to the public and houses the National Lawn Tennis Hall of Fame and Museum.

3. Bellevue Avenue

Built in 1939 for a Savannah resident, Kingscote is one of the first of the "Villas." It is an excellent example of the early Gothic style in Newport, and was designed by one of its leading proponents, Richard Upjohn. A dining room designed by McKim, Mead & White was added in 1881. The house is open to the public and is on the National Register.

4. Berkeley Villa
Bellevue Avenue (E)

Built in 1910 for Maxim Karolik, this is a good example of 20th c. Colonial Revival architecture with Palladian details. It was designed by Ogden Codman.

5. Elmcourt
Bellevue Avenue
opposite Berkeley

Built c. 1853 for Andrew Robeson, Jr., it is one of the early Gothic "villas" reminiscent of the Italian style. It was built simultaneously with another exactly like it on nearby Bowery St.

7. Edna Villa
Bellevue Avenue (W)

Built 1882-83 by McKim, Mead and White, this is an excellent example of "shingle style" architecture. Note the fine porches and attention to detail in the shinglework. The landscape and house blend together well — an architectural objective of the 80's.

6. Berkeley House
Bellevue Avenue (E)

Built 1884-85 by Stanford White, this brick house reflects the Queen Anne Revival at its zenith. It is presently owned by Charles Russell and is also known by his name.

8. Eastcourt
Bellevue Avenue &
Bellevue Court

Built in the 1880's, this is a typical "carpenter Gothic" villa. The elaborate scroll work under the gables is a trademark of this style.

9. C. H. Baldwin House
Bellevue Avenue (E)

Built 1877-78 by Potter and Robinson, N.J. architects, this house is an Americanized interpretation of the Queen Anne Revival elements. Note the use of brick, clapboards and shingles to produce a very stylized Tudor effect. This combination is unusual in the Newport architecture of the period.

10. The Elms
Bellevue Avenue (W)

Built in 1901 for Edward Berwind, coal magnate, this house was designed by Horace Trumbauer. It is modeled after the 18th c. French Chateau d'Asnieres and typifies the movement toward impressive but stiff architecture at the turn of the century. Open to the public.

11. De la Salle
Bellevue Avenue (E)

Built 1882-84 for William Weld, this rough-cut granite house was designed by Dudley Newton. The exposed stonework shows a tendency away from the uniformity of the stuccoed walls a decade earlier, but the building still has a definite Gothic air about it. In its early years, the Weld estate was known far and wide for its collection of rare plants and shrubbery.

12. Rockry Hall
Bellevue Avenue at
Narragansett (W)

Built in 1848 for Albert Sumner, this is one of the early Gothic "villas." The shingle and stone combination is typical for the period, although this particular house has been considerably altered.

13. St. Catherine Academy
Corner of Bellevue Avenue
& Narragansett (E)

This rough-cut granite house was built for William Osgood in 1887. It, and the others in this neighborhood, are not of particular architectural importance in themselves, but as a group form a 19th c. collage and should be enjoyed from this point of view.

14. Swanhurst
Bellevue Avenue at Webster
Street (W)

Built in 1851, this building is a good example of the early trend toward massive masonry structures. Even the wood trim tends toward being on the heavy side, almost as if it, too, were made of stone. Alexander McGregor, the Scottish stone-mason who is responsible for this house, also built the Perry Mill, the Newport Artillery building and parts of Fort Adams. Open by appointment.

17. Vernon Court
Bellevue Avenue (E)

Built by A. J. Hastings for Richard Gambrill in 1901, this house is a reproduction of an 18th c. French chateau. It represents the height of the eclectic movement at the turn of the 20th century, when homes had come a full cycle from the simple comfort of the colonial days. The extreme formality and grandeur of this house provided an apt setting for the social life of the times.

15. Chateau-sur-Mer
Bellevue Avenue (E)

Built in 1852 by Seth Bradford for William S. Wetmore, this is another early monumental house. It is made of Fall River granite and is not stuccoed, unusual for stone buildings of this period. Richard Morris Hunt enlarged it in 1872. At one time it belonged to George Peabody Wetmore, a governor of R.I. and has been in the Wetmore family until it was recently acquired by the Preservation Society. Open to the public.

16. Bellevue Avenue (W)

This white clapboard house with the Captain's walk on the roof is a delightful summation of Victorian elements. Probably modeled after an Italian villa, it has typical porches, bracketed windows, the familiar French mansard roof and even rustication on the facade to suggest stone.

See map on page 82 for **Bellevue Avenue — Ocean Drive**

18. Fairlawn
Bellevue Avenue
& Ruggles (E)

This Elizabethan cottage was considered
fine enough to merit attention in George C.
Mason's Newport and Its Cottages, 1875,
the architectural synopsis of the period.
Notice the excellent use of brick and
brownstone, and the fine wood trim. It is
presently part of the Vernon Court
complex.

19. Ivy Tower
Bellevue Avenue (W)

Built c. 1883, this three-story cottage has
developed the Elizabethan concept a little
further. It has a definite half-timber Tudor
exterior with rough-cut stone walls on the
first story. It is also owned by Vernon Court.

20. Sherwood
Bellevue Avenue
near Bancroft (W)

This massive Georgian mansion was built
in 1904. It is a classic study in Colonial
Revival architecture, employing every possible Palladian device. Note the columns,
window trim and massive entry. From the
back it very closely resembles the "White
House." The flagpole is the mast from the
"Resolute," 1920 America's cup defender.

22. Beechwood
Bellevue Avenue (E)

This house was built between 1851-52. Calvert Vaux and A. J. Downing collaborated on the design for this massive stuccoed brick house. It is ironic that Downing, who articulated the cottage style and anticipated the very expressive use of materials which was to come later, could have also designed a house as abstract and heavy as this one. It was partially destroyed by fire in 1855 and was rebuilt by Vaux from the original plans.

21. Rosecliff
Bellevue Avenue

Built in 1902 for Mrs. Hermann Delrichs and designed by McKim, Mead & White, Rosecliff is another palatial copy. It was modelled after the Grand Trianon at Versailles complete with formal gardens and a lavish interior. This extreme of Newport architecture is similar to Miramar, Vernon Court and other houses of the early 20th Century which verge on the theatrical. Recently given to the Preservation society by Mr. and Mrs. Edgar Monroe, the house is open to the public.

See map on page 82 for **Bellevue Avenue — Ocean Drive**

25. Beaulieu
Bellevue Avenue (E)

Built 1856-59, this house aptly states the summing up of the trend toward massive or monumental houses during the 50's. Note the stylized mansard roof, minus the Gothic peaks and gables, the exposed brick, rather than stucco surface, and the decorative treatment of the windows and porch.

23. Marble House
Bellevue Avenue (E)

This mansion was built in 1892 by Richard Morris Hunt, architect for the elite in Newport at the time, for William K. Vanderbilt. It represents the essence of his imperial architecture and the interior reflects the work of the best decorators of the times. It cost $11,000,000 to build, and the 1/2 million cubic feet of marble used in its construction was transported from New York by steamboats and cut in Newport. It was Mrs. Vanderbilt's home and the scene of lavish entertainments. Open to the public.

24. Champ Soleil
Bellevue Avenue (W)

Built in 1929 by Polhemus & Coffin, this is a stucco mansion in the popular French provincial style. The landscaping, completed in 1947, was the work of Umberto Innocenti and Richard Webel. It augmented the provincial flavor of the building with a wild rather than formal setting.

26. Clarendon Court
Bellevue Avenue (E)

Designed by Horace Trumbauer, who also did the Elms, this house was built in 1904. It was designed after an 18th century English mansion. Across the street is Rovensky Park, donated to the city by the late John Rovensky who owned Clarendon Court.

27. Thayer Cottage
Bellevue Avenue (W)

This important example of the "stick style" wooden "villa" was built in 1870. All the elements present in his house, i.e. display of framing lines with decorative "sticks," elaborate roof lines and many juxtaposed surface planes, were a fore-taste of the highly original houses to be built in the next two decades.

28. Miramar
Bellevue Avenue (E)

Built in 1914 by Horace Trumbauer, Miramar was the last of its type to be constructed in Newport. It falls somewhat short of its predecessors in scale and effect, although it is a study in adherence to the tenets of classic architecture. It presently serves as a school for girls.

See map on page 82 for **Bellevue Avenue — Ocean Drive**

29. Belcourt Castle
Bellevue Avenue (W)

Built by Richard Hunt in 1892, this house covers every architectural style, from the French hunting lodge it is patterned after, to Hunt's own earlier work in Newport during the flowering of the "stick style" houses. The interiors reflect Hunt's mood when he did this house and literally take one back to the Middle Ages. Open to the public.

30. Rough Point
Bellevue Avenue (E)

This house was built 1888-91 by Peabody and Stearns for Frederick Vanderbilt. It is a very large house in the English Tudor style. The rough-cut sandstone was a favorite material of the architects.

31. Rockhurst Gate House
Bellevue Avenue (S)

This little gatehouse is the remnant of an estate which is now gone. It is also in the Tudor tradition and serves today as a reminder of the luxury of days gone by.

32. Roselawn
Corner Bellevue (N)

This "carpenter Gothic" house was probably built in the mid-19th century. Its many-gabled roofs with lacework trim and elaborate porches is very common to the period. Later alterations have lessened the effect of this trim.

33. Inchquin
Bellevue Avenue
& Ledge Rd. (N)

Rough-cut granite is the basic material for this "villa." It is a quaint reminder of the French renaissance style so popular here during the 19th century. It is interesting to note the rather unusual tile roof.

34. Mailands
Bellevue Avenue
& Ledge Rd. (S)

This rambling Victorian house still shows the basic elements of the well developed Gothic period. In 1886 a second house was moved to the site and joined to the original building, altering the lines.

See map on page 82 for **Bellevue Avenue — Ocean Drive**

35. Beachmound
Bellevue Avenue (N)

Built by Henry I. Cobb, architect, in 1897, this is a typical example of the Colonial Revival architecture which was to become so popular in the early 20's. Note the repeated use of columns on the entry and west facade.

36. Bailey's Beach
Ocean Avenue

Bailey's Beach, south of Almy Pond, was, and still is, the center of daytime distractions for the summer colony. It marks the beginning of the famed Ocean Drive where the summer colony expanded after the turn of the century. Although the houses do not have the same architectural importance as those in Newport proper, the Drive is one of the most luxurious and beautiful seascapes anywhere in this country.

37. High Tide
Ocean Avenue (N)

Built for William Star Miller by Whitney Warren in 1900. High Tide is patterned after a provincial French chateau. The informality of its stucco and timber construction is in keeping with the rugged ocean setting.

38. The Ledges
Ocean Avenue (S)

Built for Robert Cushing in 1867, The Ledges is a large "stick style" cottage very typical of the 60's. It is presently owned by Mr. and Mrs. Howard G. Cushing.

39. Crossways
Ocean Avenue (N)

Built in 1898 by McKim, Mead and White, Crossways is a large Colonial Revival mansion, with typical Palladian detail. It was built for Mrs. Stuyvesant Fish who, along with the Vanderbilts and Astors, completed the social triumvirate of the Newport summer colony at the turn of the century.

40. Idle Hour
Ocean Avenue (N)

This French provincial house was built by Frederick R. King, architect, in 1929. It overlooks Lily Pond, a favorite skating spot and haven for wildlife. On the ocean side of the road is Hazard's Beach.

42. Little Clifton Berley
Ocean Avenue (S)

Built in 1930 by Charles Barton Keen, architect, this red brick "villa" recalls the architecture of French Normandy.

41. Near Sea
Ocean Avenue (S)

Ballantyne and Olson were the architects for this house, built in 1937. It is also French provincial in design, effectively executed in red brick.

43. Eagle's Nest
Ocean Avenue (S)

This English manor house was built 1922-24 by William Aldrich and Henry Sleeper. This house and its neighbors are built right on the edge of the sea.

44. Normandie
Ocean Avenue (S)

Built in 1914 by William A. Delano, architect, this house as the name implies is also Norman. It is a long, low one-and-a-half-story country estate, set in a brick courtyard and complete with a tile roof.

45. Seafare
Ocean Avenue (S)

William MacKenzie was the architect for this house, built in 1937. It is a large stone house, also in the prevalent French provincial style.

46. Playhouse
Ocean Avenue (S)

At one time part of a large estate, this house was built as a playhouse. If one imagines it without paint, it would be a typical Elizabethan cottage, with its bracketed roofs and ornamented style.

48. Wrentham House
Ocean Avenue (N)

49. Avalon
Ocean Avenue (N)

47. Wildacre
Ocean Avenue (S)

This house was built in 1901 for Albert Olmsted, the well-known landscape architect. It is of particular interest because it was designed by a California architect, Bernard Maybeck, for this site by long distance. It falls into the general "shingle style" with the cut-rock first story, and shingles above, but it is totally different from others in Newport. It is an excellent example of the effort to combine house and setting into a harmonious unit.

Richard Morris Hunt designed this house in 1891. It is interesting to note that Hunt was working on this excellent "shingle style" house at the same time he was building the Breakers and other Newport mansions. It is said that Hunt, near the end of his life, commented that he hoped to be remembered for his wooden houses, and not for his palaces alone.

This house has a distinct Spanish tone. It is stuccoed, with the colonade and tower one would expect in a Spanish "villa." To get a better look at Avalon and Wrentham House, it is possible to pull off the Ocean Drive into a parking area ahead.

50. Price's Neck and Ocean Drive
Ocean Avenue (S)

Here, as one rounds the bend and confronts the sea, is one of the most beautiful stretches of scenery on the island. To the left is Price's Neck and the Cove it protects. To the right is the wide mouth of Narragansett Bay. Three miles distant is the Brenton Reef Light Tower, installed in 1953. One of the first automatically controlled towers in the country it faithfully keeps ships clear of the hazardous Brenton Reef shoals. Near Jamestown is the Beavertail Lighthouse — originally erected in 1749 — America's first light-house. It has been rebuilt several times, and continues to serve as a guide for entry into the harbor. In the summer, this area of Ocean Drive is a popular picnic spot. During the America's Cup races it is lined with cars trying to glimpse the races which are held directly out to sea from here. It is also a haven for fishermen who cast off the rocks, late into the summer evenings, angling for the abundant striped bass and flounder.

Amongst the wild rosa rugosa are the remains of the old Budlong estate, The Reef, built in 1889 and abandoned to the elements for a long time. Many, many years ago the main house burned to the ground.

The state of Rhode Island recently acquired the property, including the stable, water tower and servants' house — all that remained. The entire area is under development as a park.

See map on page 82 for **Bellevue Avenue — Ocean Drive**

52. Shamrock Cliff
Ridge Road (W)

Built 1894-96 by the Boston firm, Peabody and Stearns, this cut-granite and redstone trim mansion is one of the early Drive residences. It is now maintained as a hotel and restaurant.

51. U.S. Coast Guard Station
Ridge Road (W)

The Coast Guard Station on Castle Hill was completed in 1940 as a replacement for its predecessor on Price's Neck which was washed away in the 1938 hurricane. The facility watches over Narragansett Bay and the off-shore Rhode Island area and controls the Brenton Reef Light Tower. Castle Hill is the site of the first rampart built to defend the Bay, and the Castle Hill Light, the first on this side of the Bay, still functions. Open to the public.

53. Broadlawns
Ridge Road (W)

This wooden "cottage" was built in 1882 for Josiah Low. With its mansard roof and bracketed porches, it is representative of the 80's.

54. Newport Country Club
Harrison Avenue

Off to the south can be seen the Newport Country Club, built by
Whitney Warren in 1894. It is one of the oldest golf courses in the
country.

55. Hammersmith Farm
Harrison Avenue (N)

Built in 1888 for John W. Auchincloss, this house was designed by
R. H. Robertson. It is a fine example of the late "shingle style"
architecture using a combination of stone, brick and wood. The
landscaping was done by the Olmsted Brothers who also did Central Park in New York City.

See map on page 82 for **Bellevue Avenue — Ocean Drive**

56. Brenton Farm
Harrison Avenue (N)

This little gambrel roof farmhouse was one of the early houses built on Brenton's Point. William Brenton, Governor of the Colony, had a large scale farming operation in full swing out here long before this house was built. It included the usual horses and cattle, as well as 11,000 head of sheep. In his extensive orchards he developed the first Rhode Island Greening apple.

57. Fort Adams
Harrison Avenue

A fortification at Fort Adams was completed about 1799. It was enlarged after the War of 1812, by Alexander McGregor, the Scots stonemason responsible for the Perry Mill, Swanhurst and the Artillery Company.

For years the fort remained abandoned, cut off by Navy housing. With Navy cutbacks, the state acquired the property and roads have opened the area as a park. There is a program for the restoration of the fort. During the summer the state provides tours. The area provides a grand view of summer sailing in the harbor and on the bay.

58. Edgehill
Harrison Avenue (S)

McKim, Mead, and White designed this house for George King in 1887. It is a good example of an adaptation of the "shingle style," then current, into stone. The slate and stucco touches are fairly recent.

59. Beacon Rock
Harrison Avenue (N)

This is another McKim, Mead and White house, built in 1889, in Georgian style. Its construction was the occasion of much local interest as the rock on which it was built had to be blasted away. The dynamite charges could be heard all over Newport and drew daily crowds.

60. Beachbound
Harrison Avenue (N)

This house was built in 1895 for William Burden. It was designed by Peabody and Stearns and is typical of their work with cut-granite and shingles.

61. Bonniecrest
Harrison Avenue (N)

This house was designed by John Russell Pope and was built between 1912-18. The landscaping, executed by the Olmsted Brothers, includes the greenhouses and gardens across the street. One catches only a fleeting glimpse of the house itself, a grand Elizabethan stone and brick manor house.

63. The Chalet
Halidon Avenue (E)

This house was designed by Leopold Eidlitz in 1854 and is in a class by itself. It is modeled after a Swiss chalet with several levels up and down the hill, terraces opening off many of the rooms, jagged roof lines, open lacework decoration and vertical boarding with the familiar "stick" work. This was the first house built on Halidon Hill.

62. Freidheim
Harrison Avenue (N)

This is one of the early farm houses built south of town. It has been altered considerably. At one time it was a residence of Theodore Havermeyer.

64. Harbour Court
Halidon Avenue (W)

Cram, Ferguson and Goodhue were the architects for this French chateau mansion built in 1904. The house has a commanding view of the harbor and the grounds were appropriately landscaped by the Olmsted Brothers.

65. Brooks House
Halidon Avenue (E)

This house, built during the latter half of the 19th century, has been considerably altered. It still retains the Victorian touch with its bracketed roof and balustrade.

66. Ida Lewis Yacht Club
Wellington Avenue (N)

This is one of two Yacht Clubs in Newport and is situated on the site of the Old Lime Rock Light House whose long-time keeper is honored in the annals of history for her bravery. Ida Lewis was born in Newport in 1842. In 1854 she rescued four men whose boat had capsized, beginning a career of courageous service to Newport which lasted until her death in 1911.

67. King Park
Wellington Avenue (N)

This park which looks over the busy Newport Harbor, commemorates the arrival of the French allies in 1780. The statue is Count de Rochambeau, commander of the French troops, who played such an important part in winning the American Revolution.

See map on page 82 for **Bellevue Avenue — Ocean Drive**

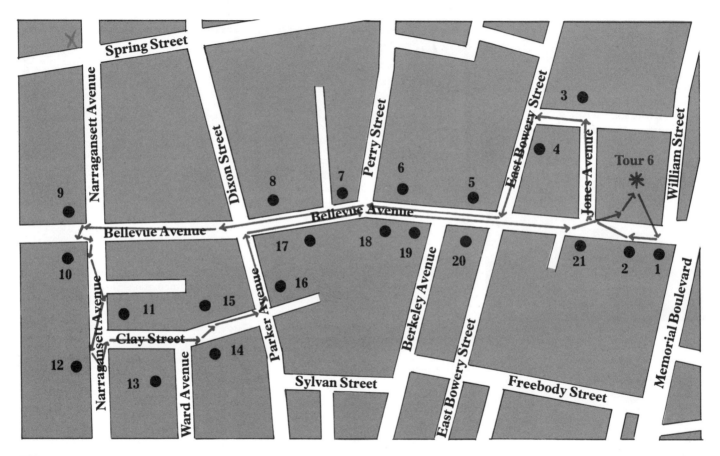

Spring Street

Narragansett Avenue

Dixon Street

Perry Street

East Bowery Street

Jones Avenue

William Street

Tour 6

Bellevue Avenue

Bellevue Avenue

Narragansett Avenue

Parker Avenue

Berkeley Avenue

East Bowery Street

Memorial Boulevard

Clay Street

Ward Avenue

Sylvan Street

Freebody Street

Tour 6
Clay Street

As one strolls the well-kept blocks in this tour, it is important to remember that although the "gilded age" is gone, Newport is still rich in after-effects. The summers are filled with social events and year round residents provide a cosmopolitan aura not found in other cities this size. New efforts are continually made to keep Newport a patron of the arts. The tradition of the early days of the Reading Room and Philosophical Clubs is not lost in the frenetic pace of the modern world.

Newport was the scene of the first Jazz Festival in 1954. While this event shocked the summer colony, it was ironically sponsored by old guard members of that same community. Recently, the same innovative spirit was shown by the introduction of the Newport Music Festival. The doors of the Preservation Society mansions were thrown open to the musicians and public alike, and strains of forgotten 19th century melodies wafted through the summer air.

The houses seen on this tour are very important in their own right. With few exceptions, they were all built during the Gothic Revival period just coming into vogue when Bellevue Avenue was first expanding southward. One house on the tour is owned and maintained by the Preservation Society, but the others are the homes of many men and women who make Newport the cultural center it is today.

1. Travers Block
    Bellevue Avenue (E)

Built c. 1875 by Richard Morris Hunt as shops with bachelor quarters above, this building was heralded by the townspeople with great anticipation. The Avenue had already begun to expand southward and there was a need for shops in this area. The half-timber construction was very popular at this time.

2. The Casino
    Bellevue Avenue (E)

This block of buildings was designed by McKim, Mead and White and built 1879-81 for James Bennett. It was said to be the result of a slight to one of Bennett's friends by members of the Reading Room Club. Bennett, piqued, had the Casino built with its own men's Club quarters where he could entertain as he pleased. It is considered to be one of McKim, Mead and White's best designs.

3. Edward King House
Aquidneck Park

Designed by Richard Upjohn and built 1845-47, this building is the classic example in Newport of the early Gothic "mass" building. Its smooth brick and brownstone walls are balanced against each other to form a harmonious whole with elaborate Italianate trim on the windows, roof and entry. For years the People's Library was housed here. Registered National Historic Landmark.

4. Kingscote
Bellevue Avenue

This is another Upjohn "villa" built in 1841. It is an excellent example of the early Gothic "villa" with its variety of roof lines, casement windows and horizontal, uniform sheathing. Kingscote is owned by the Preservation Society and open to the public, also on the National Register.

5. Elmcourt
Bellevue Avenue opp. Berkeley Avenue (W)

Built for Andrew Robeson in 1853, this yellow brick "villa" also shows the Italian influence and is one of the best examples of Tuscan revival architecture in Newport.

See map on page 108 for **Clay Street**

7. Eastcourt
Bellevue Avenue and Bel-
levue Court (W)

Built in the 1880's, this is a typical "carpenter Gothic" house. Note the elaborate trim
under the steeply patched gables. It is one of
three similar houses built on Bellevue
Court.

6. Edna Villa
Bellevue Avenue (W)

Also known as the Isaac Bell house, this
"villa" was designed by McKim, Mead and
White in 1882. It is a typical "shingle style"
cottage, done during the period when this
style was being defined and developed,
especially by this architectural firm.

8. Bellevue Avenue (W)
The Elms

The Elms is a magnificent building designed
by Horace Trumbauer for Edwin J. Berwin
in 1901. It is modeled after an 18th century
French chateau, complete with formal gardens which stretch for a full block behind
the house. It has been in the Berwin family
until recently acquired by the Preservation
Society. Open to the public, and on the
National Register.

9. Rockry Hall
Bellevue Avenue,
cor. Narragansett (W)

This Gothic "villa" was built in 1848 for Albert Sumner. Despite extensive remodeling, the house still retains the "shingle style" look.

10. St. Catherine's Academy
Bellevue Avenue, cor. Narragansett (E)

This house was built for William Osgood in 1887. The cut-granite stone was left exposed, showing the tendency away from the "mass," uniform surface prevalent earlier.

11. Gravel Court
Narragansett Avenue facing
Clay Street (W)

Probably built in the 1870's, this fine house has all the late Gothic features with a French influence. The arched porch windows, statuary and wide entry court are all refinements on the current style.

See map on page 108 for **Clay Street**

14. Ivy Lodge
12 Clay Street (E)

This typically Victorian house, despite a variety of alterations, still shows the remnants of its "stick style" heritage. The roof lines and porches are typical.

12. Bois Dore
Narragansett Avenue (S)

Charles Adams Platt was the architect for this 1927 copy of a French chateau. The stuccoed limestone walls were very popular for this style house.

13. Chepstow
Clay Street (E) facing Narragansett

This house, probably built in the 1870's or 80's, is one of the few true mansard roof houses in Newport. It still has the slight flair typical of the so-called French roof. The brick walls, painted white, are true to form for this period.

15. William Spooner House
11 Clay Street (W)

This pre-1850 house is one of the finer Greek Revival houses in town. Its gable end is set to the street with a pedimented doorway, obscured by shingles. It has two interior chimneys.

16. 12 Parker Street (N)

This house, set at an angle to the street, is probably one of the older houses in the area. It still retains its early 19th century lines despite considerable alterations and the addition of a Greek Revival porch.

17. De La Salle
Bellevue Avenue (E)

This Dudley Newton house was built 1882-84. The exposed rock walls and Gothic roof lines are typical of the last houses built entirely of stone. The solid look of the rock surface was soon to be varied with shingles.

18. C. H. Baldwin House
Bellevue Avenue (E)

A New Jersey architectural firm conceived
this house in 1887. It is Queen Anne style,
varied with the use of clapboards with brick
and shingles.

19. Berkeley House
Bellevue Avenue (E)

This red brick house was designed by Stanford White of McKim, Mead and White in
1884. It is a classic Queen Anne Revival
house, built when this style was at its zenith.

20. Berkeley Villa
   Bellevue Avenue (E)

This house was built in 1910 by Ogden Codman. It is one of the first fine Colonial Revival houses built after the turn of the century. Note the Palladian treatment of the doorway.

21. The Audrain Building
   Bellevue Avenue (E)

This block building was designed by Bruce Price. It has especially fine Spanish terra cotta scrollwork which gives it a place of its own in this block of exceptional buildings.

See map on page 108 for **Clay Street**

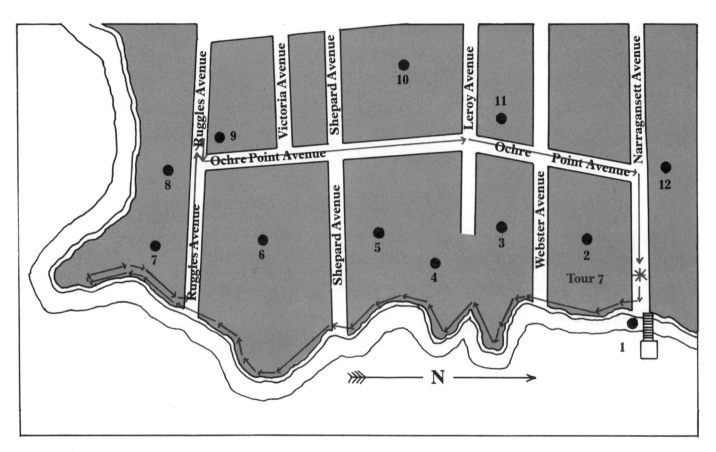

Tour 7
Cliff Walk

This tour passes over the well-trodden Cliff Walk itself. Now ravaged by neglect and the battering of the ocean, the Cliff Walk was at one point beautiful beyond description. It runs for three miles along the rocky water's edge across the property of some of the finest "villas" in Newport. It was originally a wending fisherman's footpath. When the summer colonists chose these ocean-side lots for their mansions, there was an effort to block public access to the shoreline. State law provides for this access to "toilers of the sea" however, and the new "villa" owners had no choice but to accept the invasion of their privacy. One by one "villas" included the Cliff Walk in their landscaping plans and upkeep was provided by each owner for that part of the Cliff Walk which passed over his property. Undoubtedly, there have been isolated instances where the privacy of these residences has been violated, but for the most part, "villa" owners, and cliff walkers have deported themselves harmoniously. In recent years there has been renewed interest in preserving what remains of this walk and plans for its repair are now in progress.

The houses one sees from this section of the Cliff Walk are some of the most lavish and palatial in all of Newport. There is one Victorian "cottage" literally sandwiched in its one acre plot. The others, all completed within fifteen years of each other, represent the efforts of the three architectural giants of the period — Richard Morris Hunt, McKim, Mead and White and the Boston firm of Peabody and Stearns. It is safe to say that the houses one sees here are completely representative of their work and style at this time.

On the return trip over Ochre Point Avenue more can be seen of these houses, but particular attention should be paid to the elaborate grounds. These were landscaped professionally by the best men in the field. Often the seaside frontage was left relatively unadorned, but the street side was painstakingly designed to complement the house. Probably chief among these landscape architects were the Olmsted Brothers who laid out hundreds of acres in Newport. They were the architects for Central Park in New York City and are just one more example of the talent which was attracted to Newport in the 80's and 90's.

As a footnote to this tour, it might be suggested that the Cliff Walk should be a sunny day undertaking. In the rain, or after a heavy downpour, footing can be hazardous at best.

1. Forty Steps

A fisherman's hideout, the Forty Steps was originally financed by a gentleman of means to provide easy access to the water and later rebuilt by W.P.A. At one time there was a cave at the base known as Conrad's Cave, long since washed away.

2. Southside Cliff Walk

This Queen Anne "villa" was designed in 1882 by McKim, Mead and White. It is one of the largest and best of the shingle era. The house embraces the sea with a multitude of porches and verandas and is very appropriate to its location. The plaster panel was the inventive work of Stanford White.

Ochre Court
3. Cliff Walk

Richard Morris Hunt designed this house for Ogden Goulet in 1880-91. In it he expresses his desire to go back to the basic architectural models—in this case a French chateau. This house was the forerunner for the other palatial houses he built in Newport. It is interesting to contrast its awkward grandeur with Southside which is so attuned to its setting.

Cavecliff
4. Cliff Walk

This white Victorian mansion was built in 1877. It is typical of the larger frame houses of the period with its mansard roof, although it is dwarfed by its enormous neighbors.

See map on page 118 for **Cliff Walk**

5. Vinland
Cliff Walk

This brownstone "villa" built in 1883, was designed by Peabody and Stearns. It was enlarged in 1907 by the same architects. It is the essence of the Queen Anne Revival period and, despite its size, takes one back to the English countryside.

6. The Breakers
Cliff Walk

Designed by Richard Morris Hunt and built 1892-95 by Cornelius Vanderbilt, the Breakers is a true palace. The interiors reflect the joint effort of a corps of interior designers. The grounds were done by the Olmsted Brothers. The little playhouse, seen from Ochre Point Avenue, is all that remains of the original Breakers designed by Peabody and Sterns several years earlier. The Breakers is owned by the Preservation Society, open to the public and on the National Register.

8. Fairholme
Ruggles Avenue (S)

This rambling Tudor "villa" was built in 1870 and considerably enlarged in 1930. It is a fine example of the half-timber medieval facade so popular during this Queen Anne period.

7. Anglesea
Cliff Walk and Ruggles Avenue

Detlef Lienau was the architect for this "stick style" summer "cottage." It was built 1879-80 and with its rambling roofs and facades seems to be at home with the sea.

9. Ochre Lodge
Ruggles Avenue and Ochre Point Avenue (NW)

This "villa" was built in the second half of the 19th century and exhibits all the traits common to "shingle style" houses. Note the porches and trim details, set off by the many angles of the roof line.

See map on page 118 for **Cliff Walk**

Wakehurst
10. Ochre Point Avenue (W)

This handsome house was designed by Dudley Newton and built in 1888. It is modeled after an English manor and landscaped accordingly. The best view of the house and grounds is from Lawrence Avenue.

Whiteholm Carriage House
11. Ochre Point Avenue (W)

This delightful carriage house is all that remains of the estate that was adjacent. It is a pleasant contrast to the stone "villas" on Ochre Point with its creative use of wood.

The Orchard
12. Narragansett Avenue

Built in 1871, this house was one of the early outright copies of a European manor house. The plans were obtained abroad and the result was this traditional French chateau, replete with formal grounds.

Spring Street

Mary Street

Church Street

Frank Street

Mill Street

Pelham Street

Green Street

Prospect Hill

Franklin Street

Memorial Boulevard

Fair Street

Gidley Street

Ann Street

Brewer Street

Dennison Street

Young Street

William Street

Golden Hill

Spring Street

23 22

21

20

19

18

24

28

25

26

27

17
16
15

8

14 13

12

Thames Street

Tour 8

29

America's Cup Avenue

Thames Street

9

10 11

2

4

3

5

6

7

1

Long Wharf

N

Tour 8
The Waterfront

From the first settlement in Newport, the waterfront has been the center of activity and the focus for those who lived and visited here. Long Wharf, at the foot of Washington Square, was perhaps the first wharf and grew in size and importance over the 17th and 18th centuries. North of Long Wharf was the cove which ran along Thames Street. Gradually the point at the south end of Washington Street joined Long Wharf and over the years the cove was filled. South of Long Wharf is the waterfront today.

In the late 17th and early 18th centuries, Newport was one of the important trading centers in the colonies. Mansions dotted Thames Street's east side. The west side was an active tangle of warehouses, counting houses and ship-filled docks. The extensive and lucrative trade created a life rivaled only in London and Bristol.

The trade was the Triangle Trade: slaves from Africa were brought to the Indies to work the cane plantations; sugar and molasses were shipped to New England, processed into rum and, with other products sent to Europe. As 1750 neared, the British imposed more and more trade restrictions. Perhaps it has to do with the independent nature of island people, but restrictions fueled the fire — Be damned if France and Spain were enemy to Britain, there was rum to be sold and money to be made!

With the Revolution, the term 'piracy' was often attached to the trade Newport pursued so well. The fortunes amassed made Newporters reluctant to adopt a new business style. By the turn of the century Newport had been surpassed by the ports of Boston, Salem, Providence and New York.

Through the Triangle Trade and Quaker connections in Philadelphia came wealthy travelers to whom the fine summer climate and cosmopolitan flavor of Newport was attractive. The town became the first summer resort in the colonies.

In the 19th century trade continued as illustrated by *Workday Schooners* a book of contemporary photographs taken in Newport. The 19th century vessels were coastal schooners with cargo of a mundane nature. The machine age brought mills to the waterfront, but they were not a threat to mainland operations.

Newport's growth in the 19th century was due to its redis-covery as a resort by those of newfound wealth. The harbor swelled with yachts complementing the "cottages" their owners built on Bellevue Avenue and Ocean Drive. From the thirties, when the America's Cup moved to the pleasant and favorable waters off Newport, the town has been the scene of race series involving the most prestigious yachts in the world.

On this tour, if one can overlook new roads and some modern development, glimpses of the 18th century can be seen. There are still mansion houses, a 19th century mill or two, and the harbor itself with yachts from ports around the world tied side by side with the fishing boats which ply the offshore waters.

2. Bowen's Wharf
Bowen's Wharf dates back to the early 18th century.

Elizabeth Pelham Harrison, Peter Harrison's wife, inherited a wharf and buildings from her father in 1740. The Harrisons lived in the large house at the head of the wharf on Thames Street. The wharf and buildings passed to merchants Robert Stevens and Henry Stevenson in 1783, and was known as Stevens' Wharf. In 1831 George Bowen bought the property and it remained in this family until recently, used as a service facility for ships with sail lofts, block and pump makers, a chandlery, and storage .

Preservation of the buildings and the old wharf area has been undertaken by private development.

The chandlery and the three story gambrel roof building date from the 18th century — each is built of heavy post and beam construction and each has a large windlass under its roof for hauling cargo to different floor levels. The remaining structures date from the 19th century, serving as warehouses and shops originally.

1. Perrotti Park
America's Cup Avenue and Long Wharf

Perrotti Park is a pleasant open area on the harbor which affords a splendid view of harbor activity, Newport Yacht Club and Long Wharf. It was created from land resulting from the construction of the new waterfront roadway. Design and planning of the park was done by the Urban Design Group, a Newport architectural firm.

3. The Black Pearl Tavern
Bannister's Wharf

Named after the brigantine "Black Pearl" which is home-ported in Newport, the Pearl has little architectural significance. It is typical of wharf buildings down through the years. Curtis James had a sail loft for his yacht "Aloha" here but whether in this very building is difficult to say. As a tavern the Pearl is watering spot known to yachtsmen around the world.

4. The Clarke Cooke House
Bannister's Wharf
c. 1780

Originally located on Thames Street opposite Green Street, this large gambrel roofed house was moved to Bannister's Wharf several years ago to make way for a new road. At its Thames Street location the Cooke house had suffered many abuses and changes owing to the variety of businesses occupying the building over the years. On the wharf it has been restored and adapted for use as a restaurant, creating a significant visual addition to this waterfront area.

5. The Rose
King's Dock

The Rose is a reconstruction of the original English frigate H.M.S. Rose built at Hull, Yorkshire in 1765. The original Rose was dispatched to Newport to end the smuggling operations of Newport merchants in 1774.

The reconstructed Rose is a museum exhibiting artifacts of the period.

Seaport '76, a foundation set up to run the Rose, is recreating the 64 foot sloop Providence — the first ship of the colonial navy and will lay alongside the Rose.

See map on page 126 for **The Waterfront**

6. Perry Mill Building
337 Thames Street

Built by Alexander McGregor in 1835, the Perry Mill is a fine example of nineteenth century industrial architecture. Originally the mill had a gable roof, with clerestory windows running the length of the building. The rapid growth of the textile industry in New England did not enjoy the same ready acceptance in Newport. Four mills were built in this period, two survive: the Perry Mill and the Aquidneck Mill further south on Thames Street at Howard Street. By mid-century all textile operations had ceased and the space used for a variety of enterprises over the years.

7. Ann Street Pier
Off Thames Street

Here is just a nice place to sit a bit and enjoy a good view of harbor activities. There are several town piers in Newport, but Ann Street is the only one on the downtown waterfront.

8. Francis Malbone House
Thames Street
c. 1758

The Malbone House is the only surviving example of a mid-century mansion house of this size on the waterfront. The building is a three story brick structure with a shallow hip roof. Many design features — window trim, doorway and scale — resemble the Touro Synagogue, designed by Peter Harrison. There seems to be no real evidence to link Harrison with the original design of Malbone House, just strong similarities.

In addition to the fine architectural detail of this house, the date of its construction is significant in that it reflects the well-established merchant class which existed so early in Newport. Many New England towns have buildings of similar design and size, but most date from the late 18th century and early Federal periods indicative of the later development of a strong merchant class and amassed wealth. The counting house to the right and front of the house dates from a later period.

The size and interior elegance exemplifies Malbone's position as a very successful merchant. Like many of his contemporaries, he made his considerable fortune in the early triangle trade. In the basement of the house is evidence of an underground passageway from the house to the shore. Goods traveling from ship to shore underground had the distinct advantage of avoiding the King's duties, thus creating a firm cornerstone for the building of many a Newport fortune.

See map on page 126 for **The Waterfront**

11. This is an end to the street gable roofed Greek Revival house. It serves as the ticket and information office for the Samuel Whitehorne House at 416 Thames Street.

9. 405-411 Thames Street

There must have been many commercial buildings of this style throughout the waterfront. 405 is one of the few remaining examples, built about 1835-40. It is a long two story gable-roofed building with clerestory windows at the ridge, giving it its distinctive roof profile. This style of building was a common design throughout the Greek Revival period, being used for commercial buildings as here, small mill buildings, and even row houses which were part of the mill complexes of this period.

10. 413 Thames Street

This is a good example of 1830's Greek Revival design. It has been recently restored and adapted for commercial use.

12. John Whitehorne House
428 Thames Street

Built about 1750, this house was also known as the Henry Hunter House, Hunter being the first owner. The house has a shallow hip roof with two interior chimneys, and a fine simple pedimented doorway. Inside is a central hallway running from front to back. There are rooms in each corner, many with fine original panelling. The stairway in this house is also notable.

13. 422 Thames Street

A typical gable roofed house dating from c. 1790. The pedimented fanlight doorway has interesting detail and is common for buildings of this vintage.

14. Samuel Whitehorne House
416 Thames Street

Samuel the son of John Whitehorne, built this very fine Federal mansion in 1811. The building is a three-story brick structure with hip roofs, fine trim, and an excellent doorway. The interior detailed trim is more than equal to the imposing exterior. There is a fine collection of Townsend and Goddard furniture inside and the Newport Restoration Foundation has this house and gardens open to the public year round. (Thursday through Monday by appointment 10-12 A.M. and from 2 to 4:00 P.M.)

See map on page 126 for **The Waterfront**

15. The Mansfield House
12 Dennison Street

Land records indicate a house was probably built about 1836-37 by Mansfield. He acquired a house lot which was part of the Whitehorne property and is thought to be responsible for this broad gambrel roofed cottage.

16. Horatio Tracy House
16 Dennison Street

Also part of the Whitehorne property, this two-story gable roofed house with central chimney was probably built at the same time as Number 12 just to the west.

17. 18 Dennison Street

Little is known of the early history of this house. It was recently moved to this location from 6A West Broadway. It is a two-story gable roofed half house and restoration has revealed elements which point to an early (c. 1700) construction date.

18. The King House — Gate house
Spring Street

Little information is known of this building save the fact that it was originally the gate house of the Edward King House, designed in 1847 by Richard Upjohn. Though the material of the King house is brick and the small gate house is wood the design elements are very closely related. A comparison of window trim detail, curved top doorways, and the chimney tops are just a few easily compared elements which exhibit scaled-down mirror images.

19. Nathan Hammett House
27 William Street

This is a very small gambrel roof cottage with a lean-to at the rear, thought to have been built just after 1800. Hammett and his brother each received a lot of land from their father. Records indicate they built similar houses about the same time. Brother Edward's was just to the west and was demolished for a parking lot several years ago.

20. Benjamin Hammett House
36 William Street

Somewhat larger than the neighbor across the street, this broad gambrel roofed cottage with a central chimney and simple details was built soon after 1790. This house is currently under restoration.

21. Captain John Mawdsley House
Spring Street

The Mawdsley House is interesting for what it appears to be on first glance and what is revealed beneath the facade. Under the 18th century exterior is a fine two-room, two-story gable roofed house built about 1680. This land and building were owned by Benedict Arnold. On his death it passed to his daughter, Godsgift.

She married Jireh Bull about this time. It is thought they either enlarged the house or built a new structure.

About the mid-18th century Captain John Mawsdley, a privateer and a successful man in other commercial ventures, bought the house and land. He set about creating a house suitable to his position. Another two-room two-story structure was built in front of the 17th century house. This was all tied together under a gable-on-hip-roof, a popular style for large Newport houses. What now appears to the eye is a fine 18th century mansion house with heavily molded window trim, dentil cornice, beaded clapboards and three-pedimented dormer windows. The 17th century house is revealed only by the framing and finish details of the back two rooms. The fanlight doorway is from a still later period. The house is open to the public.

22. Lyn Martin House
219 Spring Street

Martin is thought to have been the first owner of this square hip roofed house. Records show he lived there in 1777. The monitor roof is a later addition giving a rather distinguished roof line. The fanlight doorway is a very fine example.

23. Robert Brattle House
209 Spring Street

According to British listings of 1777, Robert Brattle owned this two story gambrel roof house. It was probably built after 1750 and exhibits proportions and elements common to Newport houses of this period. The recessed doorway is Greek Revival in nature, and the dormers on the roof are probably from a still later date.

24. Alboro House
41 Green Street

A whimsical collection of Victorian detail, this small house was built about 1876. Ornamented brackets, various window trimmings and a variety of shingling styles are all covered by an interesting clay tiled roof.

See map on page 126 for **The Waterfront**

25. Cahoone-Yates House
27-29 Green Street

James Cahoone and Stephen Yates built this large double house c. 1763. Each owned his own house and they remained separately owned houses until after 1850. The building is of considerable size, with an interesting row of dormer windows and doorway. It is one of several double houses still extant in Newport today and attests to the density of building in 18th century Newport.

26. Sweet House
21 Green Street

Moved to this location from Old Mill Lane in Portsmouth, this small gambrel roofed cottage does exhibit the general scale and detail of similar buildings in Newport. Built c. 1730, the house has fine interior detail and an interesting triangular chimney-fire place plan.

27. Kinsley Building
286 Thames Street

Built of cut sandstone and textured brick in 1892, the Kinsley Building is a fine example of commercial buildings popular during this period. Many of the well integrated design features draw from the emerging style theories and devices of H. H. Richardson and Hunt.

28. Commercial Buildings
Thames Street

These three 19th century commercial buildings have been included because they exhibit style and grace not found in buildings today.

The first building has had some 4x8 sheets set across the first floor but original details shine through chipped and peeling paint on the upper stories. The center three story brick building tells us it was built in 1896 with considerable attention to scale and detail. The numerous pigeons who inhabit the inner reaches of the false front cap don't seem to be bothered by its lack of paint. The building to the left is a pleasant early 19th century structure, perhaps originally a house, but over the years sympathetically changed to shop space.

29. Brick Market Place
Thames Street

Brick Market Place is one of the most recent developments in Newport. Designed by Glaser, deCastro, Vitols and Martin Adler, A.I.P. in 1974-75, the project's building program evolved from the use plan of shops, offices and residential units integrated into a relatively high density, pedestrian oriented situation. The concepts were a blend of function and contemporary planning. The varied use of wood and the irregular roof lines reflect the traditional feeling of center city density and the visual impression of Historic Hill.

See map on page 126 for **The Waterfront**

Other Points
of Interest on the Island

Outside of town there are several other landmarks worthy of note. Along the east side of the island, nestled in the Middletown countryside on Berkeley Avenue, is Whitehall, Bishop Berkeley's residence which was built upon his arrival in this country in 1729. The house gradually fell into total disrepair, even being used as a barn at one point. It has been purchased by the Colonial Dames of America and is now open to the public. A more charming country house and garden would be difficult to find anywhere. Further along East Main Road going north to Union Street is the Portsmouth Historical Society. Founded in 1938 on the 300th anniversary of the town of Portsmouth, the Society strives to preserve what remains of Portsmouth's early years. A museum is housed in this building and is open to the public. On the north side of the museum is the "Southermost Schoolhouse" which was built in 1716. It originally stood on the eastern end of Union Street, then moved to the opposite end of the street. When a new school replaced it, the old schoolhouse was bought and used as a farm building for many years before being donated to the Historical Society. It is the oldest schoolhouse in Rhode Island.

Throughout Portsmouth and the rest of the island small early graveyards dot the landscape and stone walls line the back roads and fields belying the early farming traditions. Most of the early houses in Portsmouth have been altered beyond easy recognition or destroyed, but some survive. One of the most important houses, the Overing House, or Prescott Farm, is easy to find by car. It is on West Main Road just south of Union Street. The huge gambrel roof house was the country estate of Henry Overing. The house has its place in local hearts, though, because it was here that the odious General Prescott, commander of the occupying British troops, installed himself and his staff. A certain Colonel Barton and his men stole up Narragansett Bay on a balmy July night in 1777, landed, eluded the British sentries and kidnapped the sleeping General. It was a victory for every patriot in Newport. General Prescott was later exchanged for an American general. The house is now the property of the Newport Restoration Foundation and forms an imposing visual center for the smaller local farm buildings which cluster about the small pond. All of these buildings, originally scattered about Middletown and Portsmouth, were in danger of being destroyed before acquisition by the Foundation and their relocation to the farm site. Most significant is the old Grist Mill. The Mill was built in Warren, Rhode Island c. 1812, and has been moved several times. Since restoration it is thought to be the only working windmill. When winds are sufficient, sails are bent onto the 70 foot arms and the twin stones grind out corn meal. The larger farmhouse building known as the Sweet House (c. 1710), originally stood in Middletown. The original house was probably quite small, additions creating the story and a half cape that appears today. The Country Store (c. 1700) is an early tiny simple structure which was moved here from Bristol Ferry Road, Portsmouth. The Guardhouse — early 1700's — was originally located next to the Prescott House. Its first function was probably as an out building to the farm. During General Prescott's occupation of the main house it served as a guardhouse for his troops.

The Mill, the Country Store and the guardhouse are open to the public.

Several miles north on the West Main Road, a turn west on Cory's Lane brings one to a recent acquisition of the Preservation Society named Green Animals. Green Animals is considered one of the finest topiary gardens in the country. The gardens and sculptured trees were started by Thomas Brayton in 1880 as proper and pleasing surroundings for his summer house. The house, which is also open to the public, was in the Brayton family until recently when it was donated to the Preservation Society.

On this same road is the Portsmouth Abby — a private catholic prep school. It is of architectural interest because of the very fine chapel designed by the noted architect Pietro Belluschi in 1960. Belluschi also designed the administration and science buildings at the school. All are very fine modern buildings using much local stone in their exteriors.

For anyone wishing to see more of Middletown and Portsmouth, information is available at Newport and Portsmouth Historical Societies. The Preservation Society also has information on many Newport County houses and points of interest.

Glossary

Balloon framing — refers to the use of studs instead of the large timbers which braced the colonial home. The advent of studs made a great difference as the house could assume any desired shape.

Brick bonds

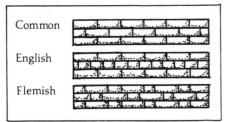

Common	
English	
Flemish	

Carpenter Gothic — refers to a house built from the standard 19th century house plans and embellished by the carpenter. The highly ornamented trim on the outside is usually the tell-tale sign. This work was only possible after the bandsaw came into use.

Classic order — pertains to the elements in architecture which draw on the ancient Greek and Roman forms. Chiefly through English influence, classic orders began to appear in the Colonies toward the second quarter of the 18th century. The most common orders are: Tuscan, Doric, Ionic, and Corinthian.

Colonial — refers to houses built during the 17th & 18th century. Strictly speaking the Colonial period ends with the Revolution, but the style lasted for many years afterwards.

Colonial Revival — synonymous with Queen Anne.

Cottage — 19th century term for the post 1850 suburban house. Both stick style and shingle style and sometimes masonry houses fell into this category. No matter that the cottages on occasion had 40 rooms. Roughly synonymous with "villa."

Dentils — small oblong blocks spaced in a band to decorate a cornice or such.

Entablature — the upper section of a classical order. It rests on the columns and usually includes the architrave, frieze, and cornice in that order. The classical details were considered an improvement on the plain trim of the early 18th century buildings.

Facade — The front or main face of a building.

Federal Period — the post-Revolutionary years in architecture. There are very few houses in Newport that are strictly Federal. Georgian is another term for the style. The houses have very simple and pure lines.

Floor plans (drawings right)

Georgian — see Federal.

Gothic Revival — supplanted Greek Revival. Scorned the cold austerity of the Greek form, related architecture to man's comfort and compatibility with nature.

Greek Revival — a return to classic Greek models after the Revolution. Although typified by the temple shaped house, the Greek Revival building could assume other forms. Columns and pedimented entries were common. Traces of this style lasted well into the 19th century.

Italianate — pertains to the Italian influence in the mid 1800's. Usually stuccoed masonry surfaces, in the stick style, with Italian ornamentation. Most of the "mass" Gothic architecture had traces of the Italian influence. Also referred to as Tuscan.

Mass — a term applied to a type of early Gothic architecture which was represented by massive buildings with masonry walls, often stuccoed. This style did not have enduring effect on later stick and shingle style work, but was a forerunner for the very late 19th century palaces.

Palladian — refers to the influence of Andrea Palladio, an Italian architect who adapted the principles of Roman architecture to his own age (16th century). He eschewed excessive ornamentation. His style was imported

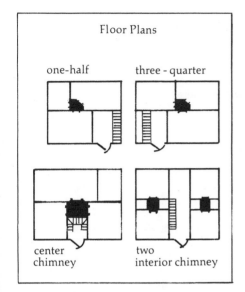

Floor Plans

one-half   three-quarter

center chimney   two interior chimney

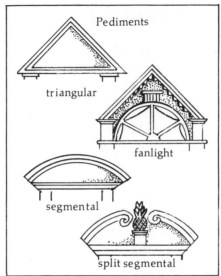

Pediments

triangular

fanlight

segmental

split segmental

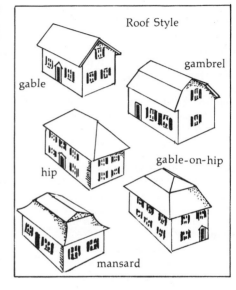

Roof Style

gable   gambrel

hip   gable-on-hip

mansard

into England by Inigo Jones. America followed suit in the 18th century. Generally speaking Palladian and classic are interchangeable terms.

Pediment — usually refers to the gable surmounting the doorway. This can take a number of forms. (see drawings)

Pilaster — a rectangular column with a capital and base, set into the facade of a building. The columnar decoration forming part

of the doorway is usually referred to as such. Early brick chimneys were often "pilastered," an extension of this definition.

Queen Anne style — In general it refers to the Colonial Revival architecture from 1880 on. Sometimes this same architecture is mistakenly referred to as Tudor. The mood was one of recapturing the comfort of the Colonial American home, but early English models for these Colonial Revival or Queen

Anne style buildings.

Roof styles (see drawings)

Rustication — channels, horizontal and vertical, cut into stone to emphasize joints. A particular case is in wood in order to effect stone.

Shingle Style — a highly developed adaptation of the Tudor English half-timber look. Shingles were used instead of slate, but the houses were usually constructed with a

143

variety of materials, brick or stone on the first level, and clapboards or shingles on the higher levels.

Stick style — denotes the trend in mid 19th century architecture to show the structure of the house in the deocrative treatment of the outside. Horizontal siding (i.e. clapboards, etc.) were replaced with vertical sheathing, usually smooth. The style also allowed a much freer house shape, a final departure from Colonial and Greek Revival ideas.

Swiss style — the basis of much post-1850 architecture was the Swiss chalet representing a return to nature. The rustic style had influence in later 19th century architecture although the Swiss style was of short duration.

Victorian — a catchall term for post-1830 architecture, but especially pertinent to the highly ornamented wooden houses of the 2nd half of the 19th century.

Villa — the 19th century house. See cottage.

Suggested Reading

The following is a partial listing of books which give a more detailed accounting of Newport architecture, Newport life, and architecture in general.

The Architectural Heritage of Newport — Downing & Scully
Early Homes of Rhode Island — Downing
Early Rhode Island Houses — Isham & Brown
Early American Houses — Isham
The Architecture of Country Houses — Andrew Downing
The Shingle Style: Architectural Theory and Design from Richardson to the Origin of Wright — Scully
Sticks and Stones — Mumford
The Brown Decades — Mumford
Early American Architecture — Morrison
Greek Revival Architecture in America — Hamlin
Peter Harrison, first American Architect — Bridenbaugh
Merchants and Mansions of Bygone Days — Elton Manuel
Newport, Our Social Capital — Van Rensselaer
This Was MY Newport — Maude Howe Elliot